game changer

ellie kildunne
game changer

With Alex Bywater

EBURY
SPOTLIGHT

EBURY SPOTLIGHT

UK | USA | Canada | Ireland | Australia
India | New Zealand | South Africa

Ebury Spotlight is part of the Penguin Random House group of companies whose addresses can be found at global.penguinrandomhouse.com

Penguin Random House UK
One Embassy Gardens, 8 Viaduct Gardens, London SW11 7BW

penguin.co.uk

First published by Ebury Spotlight in 2026

1

Copyright © Ellie Kildunne 2026
The moral right of the author has been asserted.

The publisher and author have made every effort to credit the copyright owners of any material that appears within, and will correct any omissions in subsequent editions if notified.

Penguin Random House values and supports copyright. Copyright fuels creativity, encourages diverse voices, promotes freedom of expression and supports a vibrant culture. Thank you for purchasing an authorised edition of this book and for respecting intellectual property laws by not reproducing, scanning or distributing any part of it by any means without permission. You are supporting authors and enabling Penguin Random House to continue to publish books for everyone. No part of this book may be used or reproduced in any manner for the purpose of training artificial intelligence technologies or systems. In accordance with Article 4(3) of the DSM Directive 2019/790, Penguin Random House expressly reserves this work from the text and data mining exception.

Typeset by Seagull Design

Printed and bound in Great Britain by Clays Ltd, Elcograf S.p.A.

The authorised representative in the EEA is Penguin Random House Ireland, Morrison Chambers, 32 Nassau Street, Dublin D02 YH68.

A CIP catalogue record for this book is available from the British Library

ISBN 9781529990140

Penguin Random House is committed to a sustainable future for our business, our readers and our planet. This book is made from Forest Stewardship Council® certified paper.

To all those who have been on the journey with me, those who believed in me and those who never gave up. My family, friends, coaches and more – thank you for being part of my team. We are only just getting started.

Contents

Prologue 1

1. Cops and Robbers 13
2. Prejudice 33
3. Red Rose 51
4. Teacher Trouble 69
5. Sevens Switch 81
6. Rocky Road 93
7. Final Heartbreak 113
8. England's New Dawn 131
9. Becoming an Olympian 145
10. Lukewarm Is No Good 167
11. ADHD 181
12. World Cup 193
13. Dreamland 215
14. Sports Personality and MBE 233
15. New Opportunities 249
16. The Future 259

Acknowledgements 277
Image Credits 280

Prologue

I don't get nervous for matches. I've played in two World Cup finals, but even for those I've managed to stay cool, calm and collected. I guess I'm just lucky that's my character. But as I held a tattoo gun over the wrist of my England head coach in our team room at The Lensbury Resort, the hotel in Teddington we used as our base, for once in my life I was hit with a very real sense of apprehension. John Mitchell was definitely uneasy about what was to come, too. I could feel it. His body was shaking and he had an anxious look on his face. But the fact we were in this position was entirely down to him. I was just following through on the promise he'd made.

'Mitch' – as all the girls call him – is really popular with the players. The girls love what he brings to the England team environment, both on and off the field, and he's someone I get on really well with. So, before the start of the 2025 World Cup – which was a home tournament for us – Mitch and I had a bit of fun and agreed on a bet. It was pretty simple. If we won the World Cup, I asked him, would he allow me to give him a tattoo? It was a means of motivation as much as anything else. But he shook my hand.

PROLOGUE

Was I qualified to do it? Was I heck! Hence the nerves.

When I first spoke to Mitch about the bet, he asked me if I had any tattoos. I explained that I'd got my first one – two lines inked on my wrist – a while back. I had to hide it from my parents for a long time. I didn't want them to disapprove, but I could only keep it quiet for so long. I also had the Olympic rings tattooed on my arm after playing sevens for Great Britain at the 2024 Paris Olympics.

I told Mitch the two lines meant equality. He loved that. It wasn't true. The lines mean absolutely nothing, I just thought they looked good. They're something I got for fun in New Zealand a few years ago. But it helped Mitch agree to the bet. A little white lie doesn't hurt every now and again.

So, the day after our World Cup final win over Canada on Sunday, September 28 2025, there we were at The Lensbury. We'd just returned from our team celebration at London's Battersea Power Station. It was an incredible moment. At that point, it still hadn't really dawned on us what we'd achieved, and if I'm honest, I don't think it still has fully.

The drinks had been flowing ever since the full-time whistle. But now it was the right moment to find Mitch and remind him of what we'd shaken hands on months ago. When I approached him, he was sat with his wife Jules. It's probably fair to say Jules calls the shots in that relationship. Jules is lovely, just super nice. She's very big on family, which is something Mitch has brought to the England set-up. Mitch adores her and if Jules is happy, he's happy. But, at the same time, I wouldn't want to mess with her. I went up to Mitch and said simply: 'It's time.' He thought I meant the girls were going out partying again and he offered to give me his credit card. It was an incredibly generous offer. But I didn't want his money. When I told Mitch what I really meant was that it was time for his tattoo, it was clear he'd forgotten about our agreement. And he definitely thought I was joking.

Unfortunately for him, I was in fact deadly serious. I'd had the do-it-yourself tattoo kit for a while, since the 2024 Olympics. We'd messed about with it for a bit while in Paris. But the truth is that I was far from being an expert. I'd had absolutely zero training. I was hardly going to win a tattooist of the year award. My skills were pretty basic. It meant a cowboy hat, which had become synonymous with us as an England team, was out of the question. What I *was* good at was letters and numbers.

So, that's what I decided to go with. I chose two small lines similar to mine, and the numbers 2025, to mark the year of our World Cup win. It felt appropriate and I got down to work.

Mitch was a great sport. Unfortunately, I started with the ink on a bit of a slant. Which means that when Mitch looks at his wrist in the years to come, he will need to tilt his head a bit to make the numbers look straight!

The rest of the girls all gathered round, some still wearing their medals from the night before. Jess Breach, one of my closest friends in the team, wasn't helping Mitch's mood during the process. She kept joking he'd get a sticker or a lollipop at the end, like he was a child at the doctor's. In fairness to Mitch, he took it really well. But that wasn't the end of the matter.

PROLOGUE

Bill Sweeney, the RFU chief executive, had been celebrating our World Cup win with us. He asked me, with a smile on his face, when I was giving him his tattoo. I couldn't believe what he was saying. I thought to myself: 'He must be joking.' Still, I wasn't entirely sure.

Throughout the World Cup, and definitely during the final itself, as players we kept saying to each other, 'It's all written for us.' There was a very real sense of destiny about it all. But we still had to go out there and perform. Throughout the game, I was confident we were going to win.

But when the final whistle went, it was very strange. Everything slowed down as we started to try to come to terms with the fact we'd achieved our goal – one that had been years in the making. Of course, I felt happy for myself. But what made me even more ecstatic was seeing the joy on the faces of all the other girls, the backroom staff, everyone in the stands and, of course, our families and friends. It was time to start the party.

I'm not a huge drinker, but I do like the odd glass of wine. Girls like Zoe Stratford (née Aldcroft), our captain, and scrum-half Natasha 'Mo' Hunt had given up alcohol for months to prepare for the tournament. (No one calls Natasha by her full name. She's 'Mo' to everyone, the reason being that when she was younger, that's what her little sister called her, because she couldn't say 'Natasha'.) Each to their own, but that's not my style. I'm a rule breaker at heart. If someone had told me I couldn't drink, then all I'd have wanted to do was *exactly* that. I'm a professional athlete, it's hardly like I'm going out five nights a week anyway. But my view is that the odd glass of wine isn't going to hurt my performance. I'm not suddenly going to become a bad player if I open a bottle of rosé.

The celebrations were wild. To lift the World Cup trophy in front of a sold-out Allianz Stadium was the culmination of what we'd all worked so hard for and something I never thought would have been possible when I was growing up in Yorkshire. Before the final, I'd got a little tooth cap with a rose on it made in the hope I'd be able to get it out to celebrate at the final whistle. That, a World Cup winners' medal and a Red Roses cowboy hat made for a pretty cool celebration in my opinion.

Television and media interviews followed. I can't even remember what I said. It was a complete and utter blur, with all of us players just swept along by a tidal wave of euphoria. Talking to the press is a really important part of growing women's rugby. It's something I do enjoy, but at that moment, all I wanted to do was be with my teammates.

Thankfully, I managed to get the interviews done pretty quickly and went back to the changing room. There was confetti, gold ribbon and bottles of champagne everywhere. Chaos reigned. Hannah Botterman slid across the floor on her knees, and we all wore red sunglasses with our names written on them. There was a separate area where we could have pictures taken with the trophy. But the most special moment for me came a few hours after full time when, with the Allianz Stadium stands now empty, the team went back out onto the pitch. We sang, danced in the centre circle and sprayed champagne.

It was just us.

PROLOGUE

Only a few hours before, the place had been bouncing, so the contrast was both surreal and really, really nice. Mo is the squad DJ and she's very good. But she wasn't needed at that time.

For the World Cup, our team song was 'Jar of Hearts' by Christina Perri. There's no real reason why. And it's funny when I think about it, because it's actually quite a sad song in many ways, and very slow. But there we were after winning the World Cup, belting it out like lunatics. It was perfect.

When, afterwards, I saw my mum Alison, dad Nigel, my brother Sam and all my friends, aunties and uncles who had come to the game, they were all crying their eyes out. I hadn't felt emotional until I saw them. But the sight of them bawling in the stands made me do exactly the same. Despite the tears, the room where we all came together with our families post-match was just filled with happiness. Pure, pure happiness. As Red Roses, we always say to each other that, 'We're doing this for the girls.' What we mean by that is that we want to inspire all girls, as well as boys too, with our performances. Our team is like a family, and the greatest feeling was that what we'd done had made so many other people so delighted.

The Cabbage Patch in Twickenham was our party destination. It's the most famous rugby pub in England and ahead of the World Cup it had been renamed The Red Roses Patch. It felt like an appropriate place to celebrate. We had a brief bus ride down into Twickenham. On the way, I sat next to Meg Jones. Meg and I are roommates. I admire her not just because of the way she plays, but because of her story. In 2024, Meg lost both her parents in quick succession. The strength and determination she's shown since then have really inspired both me and the team. For us to be there with medals around our necks after all she'd been through was very emotional. We were at The Cabbage Patch till the early hours. What was really nice was the fact a number of former Red Roses, like Claire Allan, joined us there.

It wasn't a ridiculously late finish for me, though Zoe and a few of the other girls went through to 6am. I knew the next day we had the Battersea Power Station celebration and I didn't want that to be a total write-off. We were up early on the Sunday morning. A few of the girls did more media duties before we headed to Battersea, which was an incredible experience. We took pictures with fans, signed autographs and lifted the trophy again. I lost track of the number of people who stopped to talk to us. I was so glad I wasn't hungover, because I wanted to enjoy and embrace every minute. It made me realise how big our success was and how much women's rugby had grown. A record crowd for a women's game of 81,885 had watched the final in the stadium, with a television audience of 5.8 million on the BBC. They were huge numbers and 24 hours later there were tens of thousands lining the streets of London to continue the celebrations with us. I remember thinking to myself at the time that this could all so easily be a dream. When we returned to The Lensbury, a few of the girls had a quick sleep. But I've never been able to nap, so powered on through, fuelled in part by the adrenaline that came from tattooing Mitch.

That Sunday night, we went to Tape – a nightclub in London. It was a chance to properly let off some steam. It's a pretty swanky place and very popular with celebrities.

Fortunately, Sadia Kabeya, our flanker, booked us a private area. Sadia knows everyone and it came in handy that night. I love Afrobeat music, so Tape – which is known for its live music and DJ sets – suited me down to the ground. But as good as all the partying was, even in the early hours of Monday morning I had what was coming next in the back of my mind: more television and radio appearances.

The RFU have been such great supporters of women's rugby and they were keen to maximise our success. I could definitely see the benefits of that. But by the Monday afternoon, I was knackered. Just totally spent. After such a high, everything had caught up with me and I needed a good sleep. That night, we had plans to go and see Lady Gaga at the O2 in London. O2 are England's shirt sponsor, so they were going to really look after us. But I just couldn't face it and headed to bed instead. My tank was empty. I pulled the sheets over me, feeling an incredible sense of satisfaction over what we'd achieved. Not one bit of me missed the concert, even if the girls who did go said Lady Gaga was incredible.

A few weeks later, when we were all back at home and the chaos was over, I went to check the post. The players all received letters from the RFU congratulating us on the World Cup success and thanking us for what we'd done. I thought that was a really nice touch. Bill Sweeney had taken the time to hand-write a personalised message at the bottom of each one. In mine, he mentioned that he was still waiting for his tattoo and was looking forward to it. It was hard for me to tell if he was joking or not.

PROLOGUE

I was all up for tattooing my coach, but doing the same to the chief executive of English rugby felt like it could be a stretch too far, even for me! Though, I guess you never know.

I've still got the tattoo gun, even if I've run out of ink. Maybe one day I'll have to get it out again ...

1
Cops and Robbers

The speed at which I can run and change direction is one of my biggest strengths on the rugby field. Stamina is another. I've been asked many times where I think those abilities come from and, of course, part of it is just genetic make-up. But I definitely think that my upbringing also played a role. I was born in Keighley, West Yorkshire, on 8 September 1999, at 1.48am. I was two weeks late and weighed 8lb 13oz. When I arrived, my parents Alison and Nigel – who were both born and bred in the area – were living in a small village just outside Keighley called Riddlesden. My parents have always had lots of close friends, two of whom were Richard and Tracey Hellawell. Richard was a radiographer and, when my mum was pregnant with me, he used my baby scans to help with when he taught students. That meant I was probably monitored more than most babies.

One day during Mum's pregnancy, Richard came to see her and said: 'I think we've found an abnormality in the scans. We think your soon-to-be-born child might have an enlarged heart.' So, after I was born, I went through lots and lots of checks, which continued through my early years. I'm told my parents were

CHAPTER 1

never really worried, even when they were in a hospital room filled with doctors, or when their daughter was being rushed away for analysis as soon as she emerged into the world. As it turned out, there was no need to be concerned. The tests always came back normal and I've gone on to live a happy, healthy and wonderful life.

Riddlesden is the place the Kildunne family has always called home. The first three years of my life were spent in a small house on a 1930s estate on Carr Lane. I don't remember that at all, as I was too young. When I was three, after my younger brother Sam was born, we moved to our forever home. It's a converted barn on an old working farm and has a big barn window and other agricultural-style features like beams throughout the house. Outside my childhood bedroom window is a cattle grid – one I remember jumping over in my early years. The house next door, where the Gaunt family lived, was also an old pig shed. My mum and dad are still there now and I hope they always will be.

While we weren't completely out in the sticks, Riddlesden has a really rural feel about it, which I still love to this day. If you want to go to the shop from ours, it's a five- to ten-minute drive. We only had two sets of neighbours, but fortunately both families had children who were around the same age as me. Jake and Adam Gaunt were brothers from one of the nearby houses, and Lily and Phoebe Pickles were sisters from the other. Initially, I was very close to the boys. But as I got older, that changed a bit and I became more friendly with the girls. We'd play together constantly. I spent the majority of my time outside playing all sorts of different games. Our favourites were cops and robbers, red arse and British bulldog. For those who might not know, red arse is a football game where the loser has to bend over and let the others kick the ball at their bum. The games we played weren't all necessarily based around sport, but mine was certainly a very active childhood. Around the house there were lots of fields – green, open spaces where we'd try and find wood to make tree houses and see what animals we could catch. We'd build chicken pens, even though we didn't have any poultry of our own. Our neighbours did have chickens, and we'd try to capture them and any other wild animals we could find.

It was just a really cool upbringing that was very outdoorsy. In reality, Keighley, the nearest big town, wasn't that far away, but it felt like it was. We very rarely went to places like the cinema or the bowling alley. Our entertainment was very much about playing with what we had around us. We never felt like we needed anything else, because we never lacked something to do.

I had Sam, of course, but for most of my early years I played with Jake and Adam. When Lily and Phoebe joined us, cops and robbers was the game we all loved the most. We'd run around constantly like headless chickens, hiding from and trying to catch each other. If you got caught and were held by the other person for three seconds, you went to 'jail' and had to go and sit on the trampoline in Jake and Adam's garden. That game definitely helped me with my evasion skills. These days, when I'm trying to dodge opposition tackles, the techniques I use aren't too dissimilar to the ones I used in the garden games of cops and robbers all those years ago. There was certainly a

CHAPTER 1

lot of wriggling involved back then and it's the same on the rugby field now.

A rural upbringing meant lots and lots of animals. At one point, we had two guinea pigs, a rabbit, two cats, a dog and a hamster. Bertie the border terrier and Albert the rescue dog are still with us now, although advancing in years. I'd often put Bertie on my back and do a few squats for some extra weight training. Chloe, a little Russian hamster, was also a favourite of mine. It was a busy home. My parents wanted us to have lots of different experiences. When I look back on it now, I feel like it's exactly the way I'd want any kids I have to grow up.

At weekends, one of the three families would host on at least one night, usually Friday or Saturday and occasionally on a Sunday. We were all very tight-knit and remain so to this day, even if time and geography has taken us to different parts of the world. I don't see the Gaunt boys as much now because I don't get to go home all that often. But the Gaunt parents – Jo and Alan – are still my parents' neighbours and I get the support of their family at England matches. Lily moved to Australia and Phoebe and their parents followed her, but we're still in regular contact.

Alongside the Gaunts and Pickleses, lots of other family friends came over. The house was always busy. We would call any family friend of my mum and dad's 'aunty' or 'uncle', even if they weren't blood relatives. Richard and Tracey were always 'Uncle Richard' and 'Aunty Tracey'. When we had visitors, we'd share dinner – a Chinese takeaway in the winter and barbecues in the summer. In the evenings, when the weather was good, we'd sit outside to watch the sun set and then go inside to watch programmes like *Britain's Got Talent* or *The X Factor*. I loved those shows. Watching people perform different forms of entertainment and become stars was something that really caught my attention, for some reason. I didn't know it at the time, but it was a sign of things to come.

West Yorkshire is a very working-class part of England. It's God's own country, but it's also not the wealthiest. In years gone by, the textile and engineering industries were the traditional providers of work in the area, but that changed long before I was born. I heard lots of people talk about the limited opportunities there were for children my age. Everyone has a different story and upbringing, but I consider myself very fortunate to have had the childhood I did and the opportunities I was given.

My mum worked in marketing and had a long stint with the bank Bradford & Bingley. My dad did sales training and worked a lot with Carphone Warehouse. These weren't typical jobs for people from the area. I wouldn't say that our family was ever sat on lots of money, but both my parents worked really, really hard to give Sam and I the lives we have had. I'll forever be grateful for that.

Neither of my parents were hugely sporty. Football was a part of our life, but we certainly didn't watch rugby at home. My dad did play rugby growing up, but not to any great level. My mum liked the game, but when she was young there was nowhere at all for girls her age to play it, so it's not something she ever got the chance to pursue. That fact makes me all the more appreciative of the career I've been able to have. Mum was

CHAPTER 1

a good tennis player, though, and her claim to fame is that she was once Keighley champion.

I asked Mum what stood out for her from my childhood. Here's what she had to say:

One thing people might not know about Ellie is her middle name is Téa. She's always been known as Ellie. Téa is a bit random, but I wanted something a little different and which stood out as a middle name for her. I think that's turned out to be pretty appropriate! People joke that I named Ellie after a cup of tea but that's definitely not the case! The accent on the 'e' of Téa is very important. I liked the American actress Téa Leoni, so that's where that came from.

Ellie was the apple of her grandmother Audrey's eye. Sadly, Audrey – who was my mum – passed away when she was just three. We always say to each other we have a star in the sky watching over her that belongs to Granny Audrey. As parents, Nigel and I always prioritised the children by aiming to give them as many different experiences as possible. I joke with Ellie that she gets some of her creative skills from me. I had quite a busy job, so I'd often bring Ellie to work with me, even when she was very young. She'd get involved in photoshoots from a very early age and was once the face of a Bradford & Bingley advertising campaign. Ellie was around marketing, photography and filming almost straight away, so I'm sure that's where she gets her interest in those things from. Ellie's always had a caring side. She was only eight when she saw on the news about a drought in Africa and barricaded herself in our outhouse in a bid to solve the crisis. In 2008, when there was that year's financial crisis and Bradford & Bingley went under, she did the same again. That hit our family very hard as I'd been with the bank for more than 20 years and it disappeared overnight. Like with the African drought, Ellie buried herself in the outhouse and said she was staying there to try and raise money to save Bradford & Bingley. It was a noble gesture, but she'd have had to still be there now to get enough funds to do that!

Sam is three years younger than me. We've always had a great relationship and it's amazing to think we've both gone from our house in Riddlesden to being rugby players. We were both always super competitive. As soon as he was old enough, Sam was out playing with me, the Gaunts and the Pickleses. He's been a major part of my life and he's definitely had an influence on the person I am today. My competitive instinct has undoubtedly come from having a younger brother who was always pushing me. Sam is different to me. I'm very extroverted. I'd say that Sam's quite introverted, though he's not shy when he's in a familiar group.

We were very, very close when we were young, even if there were plenty of good-natured scraps – the sort I'm sure all siblings get involved in. We would fight all the time, wrestling and pinning each other down. But we always had a rule that you couldn't punch or kick. We'd annoy the hell out of one another. One time, with emotions running high – no doubt over

CHAPTER 1

something completely trivial – I went to punch Sam and then I thought to myself: 'Oh no. I can't punch him because that's the rule!' So, I pulled back. The only problem was I clocked him on the nose with my elbow instead. There was blood everywhere. I said: 'Please don't tell Mum and Dad. I'll be your servant. I'll get you drinks whenever you want. You can have the TV remote.' And, in fairness to Sam, he never told Mum and Dad. That was the relationship we had. Neither of us told tales.

Mum and Dad both wanted us to be outdoorsy and create memories from an early age. Our family was fortunate to be able to travel abroad regularly for holidays. We'd go to places like Kalkan in Turkey, Crete, Egypt, and there was one memorable campervan trip to California. When I got older, we'd spend every summer in Carvoeiro on Portugal's southern coast, because my parents had friends who owned a property there. I don't think cliff jumping is a holiday pursuit a lot of families take part in, but it's something we'd do in Portugal. I've always enjoyed an adrenaline rush, and leaping into the sea from the Portuguese clifftops alongside my mum certainly provided that. I'd also climb on the roof of the house to watch the sun set with our neighbours. That and the cliff jumping weren't because I actually like heights. Far from it, in fact. I just liked the adrenaline rush they gave me.

While foreign holidays were fantastic, we'd also take short breaks in Northumberland, where we'd do sand dune surfing. And, back at home, one of our favourite activities, once we'd grown up enough for it to be safe, was going out on our family's mini quad bike. Jake and Adam's bike was much bigger but we'd go out to the lane by our houses and make ramps, then jump over them with the bikes and our scooters.

I'm now 26, but I still love going home to Riddlesden because it's a place that means so much to me. It's where everything started. I still have the same bedroom. I don't get to visit now as much as I would like, due to living down south and having a busy schedule. But, when I do, my mum does up my bedroom for me like she did when I was a kid. One of my favourite things is to go home, dig through the drawers, and look at bits of artwork and old notepads from years gone by. I guess it's the same for most children, but my bedroom was the centre of my life. I've got such vivid memories of being there.

I had a tiny little TV in my room and I'd watch Nickelodeon in the mornings before school. My favourite shows were always about mermaids! I remember listening to 'Bleeding Love' by Leona Lewis when it came out in 2007. It's very different to the sort of music I like now, but I loved that song at the time. I'd be singing it constantly. I'd also collect football magazines, ripping out all the Liverpool players and sticking them on my wall. I had a bunk bed at the time. Underneath the bed on the top bunk, I had a small little sofa and a desk. My duvet always, always had a Liverpool cover on it.

I was the biggest Liverpool fan. My whole room was Liverpool-themed and I dressed in full Liverpool kit all the time. I wore Crocs before they were cool too! I remember one game where Liverpool lost 4-1 to Arsenal and I cried so much. My love for Liverpool started from a very young age. From memory, I think it was something to do with a boy I liked at primary school.

CHAPTER 1

He supported Liverpool, so it felt like a good move for me to follow suit. The north of England is much more about football than rugby and that was the sport I got into first. Liverpool had stars like Steven Gerrard and others when I was growing up, but I loved Fernando Torres, who was my favourite player. He was a top Spanish striker and he scored goals for fun. I'd slick back my hair like Torres and wear the red Liverpool shirt with his name and number nine on the back. The slicked-back style was also partly inspired by my love of Melanie C, or 'Sporty Spice', from the Spice Girls. But it was Torres who was my first sporting icon. I don't know where that Liverpool duvet ended up. It disappeared when a double bed replaced the bunk; I would love to know what happened to it.

Continuing the football theme, we played a lot of *FIFA*. Sam and I would link our PlayStation to the one in Jake and Adam's house next door. We'd play against each other and talk through a headset. It is very common to do that now, but at the time the technology had only just arrived. We thought it was very, very cool. When Sam was playing, I sometimes used to hide underneath the bed with my iPod and record what he was saying in case he swore. I was never going to play any recording to my mum or dad. I just wanted to use it as leverage and be able to say to Sam: 'You can be my servant now because I've got you swearing on tape. You've got to go get me a drink now!'

Even at school, I was always playing games or sport with the boys. I was pretty much the only girl in every team I played in, certainly when it came to rugby. It started with Jake and Adam at home and went from there, but I never saw that as a barrier. I loved the fact I didn't fit in. That was my super strength. The boys might have said the reason they didn't tackle me was because I was a girl. But we all know it was because they probably couldn't catch me.

I went to primary school in a village called East Morton, which was about a 10-minute drive from our house in Riddlesden. It was the closest school to our home geographically, so it just made sense. Jake and Adam and Lily and Phoebe went to a different school, in Crossflatts, just down the road from East Morton, so while we still saw lots of each other outside school, we weren't educated together.

The East Morton school had something we called 'the mugger'. To this day, I've no idea why it was called that. It was just what it was known as when I arrived at the school. Essentially, 'the mugger' was a concrete court where you could play a number of different sports. You see a lot of them in public parks these days. At 'the mugger', we'd play football as well as another game we made up. The school was alongside a road, with a fence in-between, and you could see if a car was coming from about 100 metres away. When a car approached, we'd all stand at one side of the playground and then race to see if we could beat it to the other side. We'd just go back and forth at lunchtime and at breaktime racing these cars. I think it's fair to say that this game definitely helped to improve my pace.

I was cheeky, but I never got in trouble at primary school. We had house points, which were essentially a reward for doing something good. I drew a picture of a penny in year two. I put so much detail into it and was awarded star of the week. It was an

CHAPTER 1

early sign of my love for creativity. There was always a race for who could earn the most house points and I was always up there leading the way. I was very focused and well behaved.

I've recently got in touch again with my year-five teacher at East Morton, whose name is Ms Lawson. I've found I really connect with certain people, whether it's a friend, a coach or a teacher. There doesn't seem to be a rhyme or reason to it. You know when you just click with someone? I'm sure almost everyone has experienced that at some point in life. It was like that with me and Ms Lawson. That was why she got the best out of me. She was a bit younger than the other teachers and she used to keep sweets in her cupboard. If I did well, she'd say to me: 'Ellie, do you want one of the chocolates?'

Ms Lawson has come to a few of my England games in the last year, including the 2025 World Cup final. That was pretty emotional. I cried when I left East Morton because I knew I would miss her so much. As we're back in touch, I asked her what I was like in my early years at school. This is a text she sent me in response:

> You were really quiet to begin with but always worked proper hard. And then you got this confidence, which was just gorgeous to see. You used to come and stand by my desk all the time and tell me about what you did at the weekend. You always had a cheeky side and used to give a smile which meant I knew you were thinking of something.
>
> I remember one time when you set up a business giving shoulder massages, charging younger kids 50 pence

for a session. You even had to have an appointment to be booked in. That was a fun one to sort out! Your class will always be my favourite class because you were my first. Goodness knows how I managed to teach it.

Ms Lawson's message made me laugh, mainly because I definitely don't remember giving out massages.

One memory that does stand out at East Morton is from a Christingle Service when I was six. Christingle is a joyful celebration that brings families and communities together to share the light of Jesus and spread a message of hope. They can be held in any number of different ways, but in ours, a boy called Oliver Wilson and I held the two main parts. We prepared for it together. The theme of the service, in addition to the obvious religious element, was what you wanted to be when you were older. Initially, I put down that I wanted to be a footballer, because that was still what I was playing most of at the time, certainly at school. Then I changed it and just wrote that I wanted to be famous, but I didn't know what for. I think that ambition came from watching shows like *The X Factor*. Normal people became celebrities overnight after doing well on the show and I was impressed by how their lives evolved so quickly. At the time, I certainly wasn't thinking about being a rugby player! And I never wanted to be anything like an architect or a mathematician. It was always something that was on television.

Oliver and I were practising our lines when he turned to me and said: 'Ellie, I think you're going to be famous when you're older.' I'm not in touch with Oliver now, but I've never forgotten

CHAPTER 1

what he said. Oliver's words shocked me, but he made me realise other people thought I was destined for something, even at such an early age. If I'm honest, I always knew I had a certain spark. It's one of those things that's hard to describe but, if you've got it, you know about it. Even when I was very young, I wanted to make an impression on everyone and show people who I was. I had a fire in my belly. I just always knew I was different.

Initially, rugby wasn't a sport that was on my radar at all. The reason I first got into it was because one day when I was six, I was playing cops and robbers with Jake and Adam and their dad called them in because they had to go to rugby training. John Normington, one of the rugby league coaches at Keighley Albion, our local community rugby league club, was coming to pick the boys up. I just thought that I might as well go with them, because I couldn't play cops and robbers on my own. There would have been no one to run from! So, one Saturday morning, I went down to Keighley Albion with the Gaunt family; the beginning of my rugby journey. There wasn't any rugby played at East Morton. Not proper rugby anyway. There was a bit of tag here and there and always football going on in 'the mugger'. So, this was my first taste of the game and I had no idea what to expect. I didn't know the difference between rugby's two codes at the time. In truth, I knew next to nothing about either sport. It was also my first real experience of playing in a team and I loved being thrown in at the deep end and the sense of camaraderie it brought, even though I was a girl surrounded by boys.

One of the boys that I befriended that morning at Keighley Albion was called Harvey. Harvey also played at the town's union side – Keighley RUFC. I'd loved the league session so much that I was also keen to try union as soon as I could. To me, it was all just rugby, a game I'd instantly fallen in love with. Soon enough, I was playing both codes, the only girl to be doing so.

John Normington, Dean Brookes and Craig Livock were my first coaches, although at that age it was more about just having fun and getting a feel for the sport than any real, detailed practice. John, Dean and Craig had set up a young squad of boys. They'd never coached a girl before. My parents remain very friendly with John now. I was still young at this point and I don't think the coaches or the other boys knew what to expect from me. I loved the fact the other boys and teams underestimated me, because it meant I could surprise them. At first, I think they were sceptical about me playing with them, predominantly because having a girl on the team was something completely new to them. But once they'd seen me get the ball and take a run, their attitude towards me changed significantly and our relationship became very different.

For whatever reason, I clicked with rugby straight away. It felt natural to be on the pitch, swerving around attempted tackles. It was just like cops and robbers or British bulldog, only with a ball. When you're a kid and you enjoy something, you want to do it all the time, don't you? So, I kept up my rugby outside of school, alongside football. It made for very busy weekends and a lot for my mum and dad, who ferried me here, there and everywhere to matches and training. At that age, football and rugby were equally important to me. I'd play a football match on the Saturday morning, a rugby league match later on

CHAPTER 1

in the afternoon of the same day, and then a union match on the Sunday. My mum and dad were always there. Sam was too, even if he was reluctant to be. I remember Sam doing headstands on the side of the pitch, or playing on his Nintendo under his coat when the weather was cold.

Football had been my first real love, especially Torres and the rest of that Liverpool squad. While I played with boys in rugby, at Bingley Juniors, my football team, it was all girls. It was a brilliant set-up. I played as a striker – like Torres – or on the right wing. In one game, I scored 10 goals – one of which was the winner – to take the team through to a cup final. My mum still has the video tape. Before that semi-final, which was against our big rivals Guiseley, my dad said he'd give me a pound for every goal I scored if we reached the final. I'd never had so much pocket money!

By the time I was 11, I had given up rugby league. Obviously, being born and bred in the north of England, where league is huge and arguably bigger than union, I was always going to play it at some point. But there were a couple of reasons why I went down the union route. The first was that I preferred it, mainly because you touched the ball a lot more. I was a winger then, and in league you don't get many touches in that position. You only really got the ball on the sixth tackle – which is the last play of possession a team has before they have to give the ball back to the opposition, unless they score a try. I just wanted to be involved in the game by getting my hands on the ball and running. I'm the same now as when I was six or seven years old. The other thing was that in league there were a lot of fights. The older boys at Keighley Albion were barrelling and scrapping all the time.

Secondly, I felt as if union offered a better pathway for the future. Don't get me wrong, I still enjoyed league. The difference was that Keighley RUFC, where I was coached by Duncan Grant, had more games. I think I probably was already showing a bit of talent then, but more than anything I wanted to get better. So, for me, it wasn't necessarily about choosing one code over the other, I just wanted to play as much rugby as possible, and that was what Keighley RUFC could provide.

I'd been bitten by the rugby bug. I enjoyed it so much, which meant that I found it odd that I was the only girl playing. Why didn't other girls feel the same way about the sport as me? I guess that comes back to me knowing I was different. That wasn't an issue for me. It's cool to be different. All I knew at the time was that rugby union was something I wanted to continue with as I got older and progressed to senior school. Rugby in Keighley was just the start of me playing a sport that ultimately would become the central part of my life.

While it would not turn out to be straightforward, my rugby journey had begun ...

2
Prejudice

My mum and dad never intended for me to go to a private school. It wasn't something that was on their radar. But while Riddlesden was a wonderful place to grow up, the senior schools in the Keighley area weren't great at all. That worried my mum and dad, who have always believed in working hard to get the highest grades possible and wanted to give me the best chance to do that. They made that very clear to me from an early age. Initially, the plan was that after East Morton I'd go to an all-girls grammar school in Skipton.

To do so, I had to take a special entrance exam, consisting of illogical tests. Well, they were to me, anyway. I had to get private tutoring to prepare me, but, for whatever reason, I just didn't get on well with it at all. I found the work very, very hard. A lot of it was based around analysing various different shapes, really different from the exams I was used to, which tended to revolve around knowledge and learning. In some ways, it was very similar to the concussion test rugby players do after they've had a head injury on the field.

The bottom line was I didn't get into the girls' school and I'm glad because, instead, when I was 11 I went to Woodhouse

Grove. Woodhouse Grove is a private, co-educational day and boarding school and sixth form. It is located to the north of Apperley Bridge, about 40 minutes away from my home. Sending me to Woodhouse Grove was a big decision, but my parents saw it as the best option for me when compared to the other schools in the area. Their hard work made it possible and I'll be forever thankful to them for that.

I didn't want to go to Woodhouse Grove at first. I hated the idea of leaving my friends behind. But, as a family, we drew up a long list of the pros and cons, and I came round to it. I wasn't aware of it at the time, but one of the cons was the financial implications for my parents. They had good jobs, but large parts of their salaries would go on the school fees. One of the big pros was that it was a school very much built around sport, and by the age of 11, that was my focus. Outside of school, I was already playing rugby for Keighley and football for Bingley Juniors, and my parents knew Woodhouse Grove would provide sporting facilities and opportunities for me I wouldn't get elsewhere.

I was a day pupil, which meant I took the bus on route No. 2 to school. You made a lot of friends that way because it was quite a long drive. There were times my mum or dad would drive me, and when I was a bit older a train station was built outside the school, so we started getting the train. I knew only one or two people there when I started, but that was a good thing. In at the deep end.

When I first arrived, I remember sitting in the headmaster David Humphreys's office. The message from him was crystal clear – girls don't play rugby at Woodhouse Grove. He stressed that there were all sorts of other sports I could play – netball or hockey for example. I just kept saying in response: 'I play rugby.' I wasn't trying to be difficult. It was just that I knew rugby was my thing. I eventually convinced Mr Humphreys to try me out and I was put in the under-11 B team. He was going into uncharted waters with me because no girl had played rugby in the school's 200-year history. When I started, I was the first and only one.

In my first game, I scored a hat-trick and by the next week I was in the A team. It gave me real confidence that I could play rugby to a high standard, even though I was still young. A few years ago, Woodhouse Grove invited me to return to the school and talk at their annual prize day, which is quite a significant deal. They get some quite big names doing it. I was delighted to see Mr Humphreys, who was a great teacher. He was so happy that I'd achieved my dream of playing rugby, even though that was far from the norm at the school when I started there.

The sporting facilities at Woodhouse Grove were great. I had everything I needed there: multiple rugby pitches, a small gym and an indoor netball court in the sports hall. Another thing I really loved about the school was that it was relatively small. Though it was far larger than my primary school, with roughly 1,000 pupils, it wasn't so huge that you ever felt lost there. This might sound a touch odd, but I could recognise every student by looking at the backs of their heads. When someone was walking ahead of me down the school drive, I'd know exactly who it was. The school community was so tight-knit and I just knew everybody so well. It was the perfect place for me to grow not only as a young girl, but as a girl with a passion for rugby.

CHAPTER 2

I loved Woodhouse Grove and everything it did for me, but there were some ups and downs along the way. I wasn't aware of it at the time, but when I first arrived, it was definitely seen as weird that I played rugby. I never felt like that. To me, playing rugby was entirely natural. It was just what I did. But a number of things happened that, now I'm a bit older, I'm able to say weren't quite right. If I went to a sleepover at another girl's house, no one would share a bed with me because they assumed I was gay, based solely on the fact I played rugby. I was still very young at the time – about 11 or 12 – so none of us fully understood what being straight or gay meant anyway. But that wasn't an isolated incident.

Another time at school, a girl came up to me at a moment when everyone else was around, pinned me against the wall, and tried to kiss me. I've no idea of her sexuality, but it was crystal clear her aim was to see if I'd kiss her back. She wanted to prove I was a lesbian, because that's what she thought I was. Again, that was purely based on the fact I played rugby. I didn't kiss her, of course. I was like: 'What the hell is going on? I don't want to kiss ya!' I haven't ever told my parents about those incidents. I was able to brush them off because, at the time, I didn't really know what they meant. Perhaps it was the naivety of youth. It wasn't something that I ever thought of as bullying or anything like that. I just got on with it. I was quite strong-willed as a child, and still am today, which allowed me to move on pretty quickly. But I'm fully aware that if similar incidents happened to someone with a different type of character, the impact could be far greater. It's only now that I look back, I can say: 'Oh wow. That was not okay.'

At the time, I was just playing rugby and going to school. That's all I wanted to do. I didn't know about the stereotypes around women's rugby, or even what a lesbian was. That wasn't something I'd ever thought about anyway because I knew from very early on in my life that I fancied boys. I knew I didn't want to kiss any of the girls. The incidents weren't anything I ever felt sad about. I think I just felt confused. I couldn't get my head around why no one at my new school wanted to share a bed with me at a sleepover. It's often assumed that it's boys who pick on others at school or act as bullies. My experiences have shown me that's not always the case.

Reliving these stories here does make me upset, mainly because I wouldn't want other people to go through similar experiences. When I started at Woodhouse Grove, there were people who were still questioning what a female rugby player was and what a girl playing rugby meant. Thankfully, it is now far more commonly accepted that women play rugby, though I also know that, unfortunately, barriers and similar issues to the ones I experienced still do exist for young girls. The reason I know that is because I've heard about them first hand. I get a lot of messages on social media from young girls who have been bullied or discriminated against because they play rugby. I've also had people tell me similar stories in person. My message to anyone reading this is to just accept people for who they are and where they've come from. Don't assume anything about anyone. I've been on the wrong end of assumptions in the past. With the increased visibility of women's rugby in the world today, girls playing the game is now far more normalised. Clearly, that can only be a good thing.

CHAPTER 2

I'd also like to think that in 2026, girls can play rugby without someone making an assumption about their sexuality. A number of my teammates are gay. Others are straight. It doesn't matter to me whatsoever. In society, we need to accept everyone for who they are. Yes, progress has been made on that front. But there is more still that can be done until we have a truly open and accepting society.

There was never any danger of my experiences holding me back and some of my closest friends to this day are ones I met first at Woodhouse Grove. I'm still very close with Morgan Halliday, Rachael du Plessis, Poppy Wilson and Maisie Dixon. We find it funny that those girls – Maise and Poppy apart – weren't sporty at all. They all still come to watch my games with England.

I got on well with all the teachers at Woodhouse Grove, except for one. I was still cheeky, as I was at East Morton. I was often on the cusp of trouble, but never really in it. It's the same now, when I'm on the rugby field. I often say a few words or sometimes get a telling-off from the referee, but I rarely get yellow carded or anything like that. I enjoyed school and did well on the whole. I was in set one for most things and I worked very hard for my GCSEs.

My problem was I didn't always listen as much as I should have. I would always be talking and distracting other people. That didn't endear me to my maths teacher. She didn't like that I was a chatterbox. It's true I did talk a lot. But I still did all my work.

I used to hate being sat at the front of the class, because I'd turn around all the time and get distracted. My favourite position was to be at the back of the class, so I could see everything going on in front of me. I would try to tell the maths teacher that and she would just send me out of the room all the time. I was put on a report card. One day, we all came into the maths lesson and the teacher said: 'Everyone stand up, we're going to change our seating plan.' I thought to myself: 'At last!' The teacher went around everyone and asked: 'Where do you want to sit and who do you want to sit next to?' When it got to what I thought was going to be my turn, she left me out. I was then boxed in alongside the Chinese boarding students, who didn't speak any English. I don't know if it was a way of trying to get me to concentrate, but it didn't work because I'd start playing with the translator the Chinese pupils had to help with their schoolwork.

So, then I got sent to the front of the class. And when I say the front of the class, I don't mean the front row alongside other pupils. I was up against the blackboard and the teacher was behind me. I wasn't allowed to turn around when she was talking. That really didn't help me at all. If somebody puts me in a box, I'll just fight to get out of it. I'm like that as a player now. If I'm surrounded by tacklers on the field or in a tight space, I'll try my best to get out of it. I don't like being constrained. I like to feel free. Eventually, I did escape that situation, as I ended up doing maths in my own classroom across the hall. I was put there so I couldn't distract anybody, which was what I'd been up to in the main class. I loved that, because I played music all the time. I was there for about four months. Whenever one of my classmates went out to go to the toilet, they'd come to my room. It was the place to be!

But I did find the experience quite stressful. I went through a phase in school where I'd have mini panic attacks. My skin would get really itchy. I'd get really hot and flushed and I'd have to leave the classroom. It was my first experience of the impact of stress and an example of something I know many other young people have experienced. I thought my symptoms were something to do with my tights. I used to run to the bathroom and take them off because I thought they were too thick and overstimulating. It was nothing to do with that at all. I felt hot and flushed because I was worried and anxious in school about doing as best as I could. In the end, I did end up getting an A in GCSE maths, so the final result wasn't too bad at all.

As well as playing at Keighley outside of school, I was the only girl in the year seven boys' rugby team at Woodhouse Grove. In my second year, I continued to play with the year seven team. At that age, the boys were growing fast and I wasn't sure I wanted to tackle them anyway.

It was while I was playing down a year for the school team that I went to a 10-a-side tournament near Skipton. I scored a lot of tries that day and a number of the opposition coaches complained. I was subsequently told by the RFU I wasn't allowed to play a year down any more, even though doing so was permitted under the rules. That was because it was deemed unfair for me to play because of the number of tries I'd scored. All records of me playing in those games had to be scrubbed because of the complaints. I was left at a crossroads, one which I think many young girls often still find themselves in today. Things are changing for the better, but it is at around 13 years old that I think girls who are playing rugby start to see their opportunities become more limited. That certainly happened to me. I wasn't allowed to play down a year with the boys and I couldn't play with boys my own age for safety reasons, as they were getting a lot bigger all of a sudden. On top of that, there were very few local clubs where girls played.

When I stopped playing with the boys, my dad drove me to a girls' team in Wharfedale, which was about 40 minutes from home. It was a long trip and a significant commitment. At Wharfedale the coaching was very basic, focusing on things like how to put your hands up and catch the ball. I was past that level by then. The standard wasn't great and we didn't even have enough to make up a team because there were only about 10 girls that would ever show up. My dad would still take me to training week in, week out, to try and get me the action I craved, but the truth is I did fall out of love with rugby a little bit at that point – mainly due to a lack of opportunities.

I was still playing football at the time with Bingley Juniors and because that was all girls and there were regular matches, it all of a sudden became a bit more straightforward than rugby.

I moved to Farsley Celtic Juniors, who had a great girls' football team; I wanted to play at a higher standard than was on offer at Bingley. At Farsley, we won the national championships, but our best result was when we travelled to Manchester City's Etihad training campus and beat the Premier League giant's academy side 7-1. I loved football and I think I had the ability to continue with the game. I had trials for Bradford City, who were interested in signing me, but only on the proviso I didn't play

CHAPTER 2

rugby at all. If I'm honest, that wasn't ever really an option for me, even if football was more my focus at the time.

Even though there was no clear pathway to progressing in rugby, and football provided the easier route, there was really only one sport that was calling me. It's hard to pinpoint why. I just had a feeling that, for whatever reason, rugby was the way to go. Even if routes A, B and C for continuing with it were shut off to me, I was determined to try X, Y and Z. That's the message I want to send to anyone reading this. Don't let setbacks stop you. If one road is blocked to the destination you want to go to, don't give up. Seek an alternative option. I want to show people that you can always make your dreams come true. There is always an opportunity out there, it's just that sometimes you have to try and forge your own path to get there. With the help of my mum, that's exactly what I did.

By this point, my brother Sam had followed me to Woodhouse Grove. I remember one incident when he was in year seven and I was in year ten. I heard through the school grapevine that someone had picked on him. So, I went down to the year seven locker room and asked where the bully was. I didn't try to hurt him or anything like that. I just told him to pick on someone his own size. I'll always be protective of my brother and that's still the case, even though he's now much bigger physically than I am. Equally, I know he's very protective of me. It was never really something he showed that much, but he's always had it in him. He can handle himself and we've both had each other's backs from when we were very young.

By then, I'd had about a year or so away from rugby, but my parents continued to try and find a place for me to play.

They weren't pushy by any stretch of the imagination. They just wanted to help me find a way to pursue the sport they knew I loved. At one point, we heard another girl in the area had been given special dispensation to play with the boys, but we weren't sure if it was true.

When I was 14, my mum found out from an advertisement on Facebook that there were trials for Yorkshire County's girls' rugby team. This was a big moment, so once we found out where and when they were, of course I showed up. When I arrived with my mum, I was asked what team I played for. This was a problem, mainly because at that time I did not have a rugby side. I don't remember exactly what I said to the man on the door that day. But it was something like 'Keighley Queens'. Whatever it was, I made it up on the spot and was then allowed to play in the trials. I must have done okay because when the trial came to an end, the coaches called me over. They said: 'Look, Ellie. We know you don't play for Keighley Queens – it's a made-up team.' I thought to myself: 'I'm in trouble here!'

What happened next surprised me. I was told: 'We want you to go to play for West Park because you have made the Yorkshire squad and you're a brilliant player.' The majority of the girls who were at that trial played at either West Park or Castleford, which is why the coaches suggested I do likewise. The aim was to get me to play with a better quality of player, more regularly. This was music to my ears. After a year or two of frustration, I could finally see light at the end of my rugby tunnel.

I didn't look back from there. I joined West Park's under-15s team and was also playing for Yorkshire at the same age group level, even though I was still under the age bracket. A year or so later, I also made the under-15 team for the North of England, which was another step in the right direction. Although West Park were my regular team at that point, I also played a handful of games for Castleford in the years that followed, just to play as much rugby as I could. It was there that I first met Simon Middleton, who would go on to be my England coach. 'Midds' as he became known to me a few years later, was a Castleford man and his daughter Cara played for the girls' team there too. At the time, West Park were one of just four junior girls' teams in the whole of West Yorkshire.

The next stage of my development was a key one. I was invited to represent the North of England and play in a sevens tournament in the Sainsbury's School Games. It was under-18-level rugby. I had only just turned 15 at the time, so it was a big step up. I was playing two age groups above mine. The players that were going to be there were the best in the country – people I'd heard about but not seen in person. That excited me. I didn't fear making that leap. Holly Aitchison, who is also from the north, was on my team. Holly is a couple of years older than me and was already a quality, quality player. I really looked up to her.

Going to that tournament suddenly ignited a fire in me. Up to that point, I'd always been one of the better players in the teams I'd been in. Playing with more talented players definitely spurred me on. At those Games we had matches against teams from the south who had players like Zoe Harrison, Jess Breach and Sarah Bern, among others. Essentially, that tournament featured large numbers of girls who are now my England teammates. Being young and inquisitive, one question kept recurring in my mind – where do all these girls play their rugby on a weekly basis? When I asked, one common answer came back: Hartpury College. I wasn't entirely sure where Hartpury was. But, from that moment on, there was only one thing I could think about. I simply had to go to Hartpury College, which, I discovered, is near Gloucester. My mind had been made up. I instantly saw Hartpury as the place that would help me fulfil my rugby dream.

Once I get something in my brain and focus on it, I become very driven and this was a good example of that. I came away from that tournament begging my mum to allow me to go to Hartpury. She did not want me to, because it would involve me leaving home at 16 to move hundreds of miles away. No parent wants their son or daughter to choose to do that. It was a really tough time for us as a family, because I was set on the move and my parents certainly had reservations. At the time, I didn't know why it was such a big deal for them, especially my mum. But looking back on it now, I can totally understand.

Before I could think about Hartpury in detail, though, I had to pass my GCSEs at Woodhouse Grove. With Mum's help, I revised constantly. I had this book that had all my revision notes in it, and by the time it got to the exam weeks, other pupils were asking me what the answers would be to various questions. They'd worked out by that point that I just knew.

But, unfortunately, ahead of my crucial exams, our family was shocked by illness. My Grandma Julie, who is my dad's mum, had been a big supporter of my sporting career to that point. She helped my mum and dad with logistics around the travel to matches, often looking after me. Just before my GCSEs, Grandma Julie had an awful stroke. It was really sad because she was still quite young and had always been the life and soul of any room she was in. My mum still has the video footage of me trying out magic tricks on her. All of a sudden, Grandma Julie wasn't the same person and she had to go into a care home. She was a huge, huge part of my childhood, and while she is still alive today, her stroke hit our family, especially my dad, hard.

It was a difficult time, but I'd done loads of revision for my GCSEs and it paid off. I did really well in the exams, receiving all As and A*s in my chosen subjects. I was delighted. In the build-up to my GCSEs, my mum had relented and said we could go down to visit Hartpury College, which is a three-and-a-half-hour drive away from home. The facilities at Hartpury were amazing. I was just thinking 'wow' to myself as I was shown around. To try and seal a place there, I had to do a rugby trial and prove I was talented enough to make the team. If I wasn't deemed good enough at the game I loved, I wouldn't be going. It was as simple as that. I was really, really nervous, because I wanted to go so badly. But I spent most of the journey home upset because I thought I'd fluffed it. That wasn't because I lacked confidence. It was because, for the first time, there were other girls on the pitch that were just as good as me and I felt I hadn't done enough to stand out – something I'd become used to doing back at home. I cried all the way to Yorkshire, convinced I hadn't made it. By that stage, I was already making sacrifices outside of rugby to help me perform as well as I could. I remember leaving my friend's end-of-school party early because I had a tournament the next day. I was prepared to do things like that to be successful, but the way the trial went made me think that maybe even this wasn't enough, and that my Hartpury dream was dead.

But, a few days later I was in a physics class back at Woodhouse Grove and received the news via email I could go to Hartpury, because I'd made their rugby team. I couldn't have been happier but, for my parents, the feeling was very different.

Here's how my mum Alison remembers that time:

Ellie's interest in moving to Hartpury absolutely broke my heart. It was such a big debate in the family because it just came out of nowhere on the back of that Schools Games.

I don't think we're old fashioned in our views, but there was a nervousness from our point of view that Ellie had got a great education at Woodhouse Grove and good GCSEs.

She'd not only done really well at school, but was happy at home and had a great circle of friends. She loved life in Yorkshire and now, all of a sudden, she wanted to leave at just 16 to go to a remote place near Gloucester to pursue rugby. We were fully supportive of Ellie's rugby, but at that time there still wasn't an avenue to explore in terms of playing the sport professionally as a woman. At that point, you couldn't earn a living from doing so. As parents, that was really hard for us. Nigel and I are both from working-class backgrounds and had fantastic parents who worked bloody hard. The whole ethos we passed on to Ellie and Sam was to

CHAPTER 2

do the same – work hard at everything and get good qualifications. As such, the idea of putting that at risk by moving away from home was alien to us. But at the same time, we could also tell it was something Ellie wanted to do more than anything and Hartpury seemed like a good option in terms of balancing ongoing academic studies with her rugby. We struck a deal.

Ellie could go to Hartpury as long as she came home every weekend and didn't allow her classwork to fall behind at the expense of rugby. Ellie couldn't drive when she first went to Hartpury, so we'd often make the journey down to drop her off or pick her up. I'd cry all the way. As a parent, it's wonderful when your children get to the age where they want to spread their wings. But Ellie moving to Hartpury was not only a big moment for her, but also our whole family. It was particularly big for Sam because he was still only 13 when Ellie left.

So, that was that. At the end of year 11, aged just 16, I moved away from home for the first time, for a new adventure down south. I didn't know it then, but I would never return – not permanently anyway. Soon enough, I would be going from a school rugby player to a full England international.

3
Red Rose

When I arrived at Hartpury College, my overriding emotion was one of excitement. There weren't any real nerves or worries about going somewhere totally new. Over the past couple of years, I'd done a training camp with the North of England team and gone away on trips with some age-group rugby teams. To me, they'd felt like sleepovers with some rugby thrown in. That suited me to a tee. Moving to Hartpury was like another big rugby sleepover, only a more permanent one.

I'd agreed with my parents I would go home every weekend, but I didn't miss Yorkshire that much while I was away. My mum would probably hate me for saying that. But the reality was I was just so excited to be playing consistent and high-quality rugby in a new environment; that was my sole focus. It only took a matter of weeks to settle in. I absolutely loved it.

My birthday is on 8 September, so I turned 17 just after I started at Hartpury and could begin to learn to drive. But before I passed my test, I'd get the train back home to Yorkshire at the end of each week. They were long journeys. I'd go from Gloucester to Birmingham New Street and then change there to head to the north. There were plenty of times I wouldn't get a seat and I'd

CHAPTER 3

be sat on my arse in the bit between the carriages for three and a half hours or more. I learned to drive pretty quickly, mainly to avoid the misery of the train, and I was soon doing three- or four-hour journeys back to Riddlesden. My first car was a dark blue Volkswagen Polo. I loved that little thing. It was a great car. One morning I woke up to find it parked outside our house – Mum and Dad had bought it for me. I could not believe it.

In the first year at Hartpury, all the students studying for A-levels, like me, stayed together. If you were working towards a BTEC qualification, you had your own room to reflect your more adult status. I shared a room with a girl called Eloise Hayward, who also played rugby. Eloise and I were very different. She was so neat and tidy and I'm not like that at all. On my side of the room, I had a disco ball on the ceiling and created a balloon wall with fairy lights behind it. We used to have big sleepovers where we'd push the beds together and invite people from other rooms to stay over. If anyone wanted to come into our room at any point, I made them do a karaoke song to gain entrance. When I look back on it now, it was maybe a bit mean. If anyone got nervous about their performance, I gave them a sleeping mask that they could put on while singing their song. The reason I did that was to show people that there's no such thing as embarrassment and to help them to feel confident performing, without the worry of seeing what people thought of them. It was well intentioned, but, if I reflect a bit today, I think maybe people thought, 'What is this bully doing?'

My closest friends in my first year were two girls in the year above me – Ella Wyrwas and Rosanna Moynihan. I was so close to Ella and Rosanna but then, all of a sudden, I started thinking: 'Oh my God, in six months, they're going to leave to go to university.' I got really down about the fact that they were leaving, so much so that I ruined the three or four months that followed for myself. What I should have done was just enjoy the moment and not spoil the time we had left, but I didn't know any better then. Ella and I were very tight at Hartpury and still are today. She's gone on to play professional rugby too, and is currently with Saracens as a scrum-half. Ella has also played for England.

When I was in my first year at Hartpury and Ella was in her second, we were invited to play for a sevens team made up of some of the country's most promising talent. That side was all about developing young women's players. We'd go down to Bisham Abbey – which was then England women's training centre – near Marlow in Buckinghamshire and train with the England sevens girls, though initially I didn't have the dispensation to do full contact with them because I was still under 18. I was told I could do every part of the session other than the tackling. Neither Ella nor I was able to drive at the time, so we used to wake up at half four in the morning and get a train from Gloucester to Swindon. Susie Appleby, a legendary women's rugby coach, would then pick us up and take us across to Bisham Abbey for the day. It was a big commitment, but it was the chance to train with England players, which was unbelievable when I was still so young. It was an opportunity I was never, ever going to turn down, even though the crack-of-dawn alarm call did not marry up very well with the fact I'm not a morning person. One of the highlights of playing sevens around that time was a trip to Las Vegas. Both Ella and I were invited to play for a team out there, so off we went to the desert. In many ways it was a very random and weird experience, as we played both with and against locals, some of whom I've stayed in touch with. But it's certainly a trip I'll never forget.

In my first year at Hartpury, I started by playing for the college rugby team with the aim of progressing to the senior Gloucester-Hartpury side, who played in the top division of women's rugby in England. That would happen sooner than I thought but, to start with, I was also keen to keep playing football. I kept my side of the bargain with my parents by going back to Yorkshire each weekend and when back at home I'd still turn out for Farsley Celtic Juniors.

As a player, my speed has always been a real point of difference. And at Hartpury, even though I was surrounded by other girls of real quality, I still managed to stand out with my speed and skills. I loved it. Suddenly, I was part of something that resembled a professional set-up. I had to learn very quickly that rugby's not just about turning up on a Saturday and playing a match. There is far, far more to it than that. In Yorkshire, I didn't go to the gym at all. I trained on a Wednesday night and played on a Saturday. But at college, it was a proper rugby environment with morning training, weights, and strength and conditioning. Our digs were at the top of a hill and I lost track of the amount of times I had to sprint down it in my studs for the 6am session because I'd slept through my alarm and was running late.

LJ Lewis, who is now involved with England under-20s, was the coach. She was very strict and took no nonsense, particularly when I first arrived. She's an ex-cage fighter and her ring name was 'Big Rig', which tells you everything. She was a fearsome coach. If I was late, LJ would send me on laps of the pitch. The same would happen if I was laughing or messing about, she would say: 'Ellie. Laps.' Other times, if I'd fallen behind with my schoolwork, LJ would call me into her office, shut the door, and tell me to get on with it, as a means of motivating me. Because she was a no-nonsense character, I always did as I was told. LJ ran a very tight ship.

Hartpury was all about an early exposure to what it would be like when (hopefully) I reached the highest level in rugby. I did still try to have a laugh, though. If things are serious all the time, I have to try and lighten the mood. In my first year I had a bet with one of the other girls to see who could get through the gym session doing the least amount of exercise and without getting caught. That was fun for a brief moment, but in truth I was beginning to realise that I needed to be a lot, lot stronger. There was, surprisingly, a reason why the coaches wanted us to improve in the gym.

I only played a handful of games for Hartpury College before I was called up to play for Gloucester-Hartpury. It was a big moment because I was still only 17 and all of a sudden I was training with and playing against fully grown women. Top-quality, experienced players like Rachel Lund and Ceri Large were part of that set-up. So too was Tatyana Heard, who would become a teammate of mine with England in the future. Abi Burton, who was a bit younger, arrived soon after me. Playing for Gloucester-Hartpury was, undoubtedly, a big

CHAPTER 3

step up. I got absolutely walloped by some of the older girls in my first few training sessions. There was no mercy given and it instantly made me very aware of my physical weaknesses. From that moment on, I started to take the gym far more seriously.

It was definitely a shock to the system. Another early lesson was that I couldn't just dummy and run every time. That had been my trademark move growing up. Now, against bigger and better players, I'd look to dummy and run, but instead of finding space, I'd just get smashed. In order to survive I had to very quickly find alternative ways of playing. I didn't understand it at the time, but that turned out to be a good thing. You can't be a one-trick pony.

Not long after starting at Hartpury, I had a trial with England under-20s. I did the trial but within days I was told I wouldn't be selected for the team. I thought to myself: 'S***. This isn't good.' I'd managed to convince my mum to let me move south on my own to progress my rugby, but now I was being told I wasn't good enough to make the under-20 squad. What I didn't know was that the reason I wasn't being picked by the under-20s was because England wanted me to come into their senior training squad ahead of the 2017 November Tests. England had been tracking me for a while with a view to bringing me into their system when the time was right.

When Midds told me that he wanted me for the senior side, it was one of the proudest moments of my life, but it took me several hours to compute it all properly. My rugby had progressed at such an unexpected rate that it had caught everyone – including me – by total surprise. Looking back on that time now, it was a huge moment.

But I just rode that wave of emotion and didn't overthink things. I remember a training session at that first England camp. Midds said to me: 'We're going to do this play where we'll get the ball to the edge and when you get it, go down and just present it.' What Midds meant was he wanted to me to fake being tackled, and then protect the ball with my body while positioning the ball so that my teammates could pick it up and the next play could begin. Instead, when the ball got to me, I kicked it, chased after it, and reclaimed it. It was pretty much the exact opposite of what I'd been told to do. I don't know why. It was probably just instinct. I executed the skill well, but it wasn't what Midds had in mind. After I'd done it, I heard him going absolutely mad. He was shouting: 'Ellie, that's not what we're doing here! That's not the drill! If you want to do that, you can go back to Hartpury!' The next time we did the drill, the girls said to me: 'Just go down and present the ball.' So, that is what I did.

There were many other experiences with England that were totally new to me, including being involved in analysis meetings. All the girls would bring a notebook and, at first, I didn't have one. It's funny looking back at that, as now I like to make a lot of notes. But at the time, the girls would ask me: 'Have you not got a notebook?' I'd reply: 'No. It's all in my head.' However, the discussions we had about things like tactics, training schedules, specific moves and the strengths and weaknesses of the opposition weren't sticking in my mind at all. I had to learn the backs' moves with Scott Bemand, who was the England attack coach at

CHAPTER 3

the time, by using little packets of salt on the table. Each packet would represent a player, and Scott would move them around to show me where and when we should make our runs.

Nolli Waterman and Rachael Burford, who were experienced members of the squad, told me to get a notebook, but initially I still preferred the salt packets. Eventually, though, I realised I needed one and from then onwards it was key to my preparation.

With Hartpury, we had a professional-type set-up but we never really had meetings. England was very different. I'd totally missed the step of playing for the under-20s. It's at that level you're supposed to learn things like the need to take a notepad to meetings. I didn't know any of that because, aside from a few games for Gloucester-Hartpury, England was my first experience in senior rugby. Here's an insight into how naive I was. At the time, I didn't even know what a yellow card was or what happened if you got one. If you are yellow-carded in rugby, it means you have to spend 10 minutes off the field in what's called the 'sin bin'. It's a punishment for your crime. If you're shown two yellow cards or a straight red card, you are sent off the field permanently. The first time I played at Allianz Stadium a few months later, I got yellow-carded and there's this video of me looking at the referee and the referee returning my stare. I wasn't sure what to do.

You don't have yellow cards in age-group rugby, so I'd never been carded before. The truth is I hadn't even watched that much 15-a-side rugby. I was told by the coaches I needed to stop watching sevens and watch the 15s in order to try and aid my development in the longer, much more complicated form of the game. I could watch sevens all day at that point, but it wasn't helping my game. I wasn't as clued-up as I needed to be on things like where to stand at scrums and line-outs and the required tactics. There was still a lot of learning for me to do.

I made my full senior England debut against Canada on 17 November 2017 at Stone X Stadium – the home of Saracens. I had just turned 18 and had progressed into my second year at college. I'd gone from playing for a girls' team in Yorkshire that wasn't very good, to playing for Hartpury, where the players were better, to then playing for England. There was nothing in-between. I made big jumps and I made them quickly, too.

In my second year at Hartpury, I was living in an over-18 block and had my own room, but rugby had quickly become the full focus, definitely ahead of my studying. Midds picked me on the bench against Canada as full-back cover. That's a funny story in itself. When he brought me into the squad, I mainly played as an outside centre for both Hartpury College and Gloucester-Hartpury. Before that, I'd played on the wing. I'd had a couple of games at full-back, but it was far from a position I felt comfortable in. When Midds and the rest of the England coaches said to me they'd seen me play at No. 15 and in midfield, I thought it was too late to say anything, so I just went with it. Talk about fake it until you make it!

The Canada game was the first since the team had been beaten by New Zealand in the final of that year's World Cup a few months previously. My inexperience and lack of knowledge at that time are best summed up by the fact I didn't even watch that World Cup. I loved rugby, but I loved it with a ball in my hand. I didn't want to be sat in front of a TV watching it. I hadn't watched England at that tournament, but now I was playing for them.

There were several other new girls who came in at the same time as me – Jess Breach, Zoe Harrison, Abby Dow and Hannah Botterman, all older than me. Because I was the youngest in the squad when I joined England, I had to carry a toy lion around with me. It's a way of building team morale and getting the new players involved in the squad atmosphere. The same thing happens on a men's British & Irish Lions tour: if you lose the lion, you're punished with a forfeit. It's not a thing we do with England now, but it was a responsibility I had on my first camp. I had to take it everywhere with me – dinner, team meetings, training. But my problem was I'd leave it behind all the time. Even when I didn't, the girls would steal it to try and make my life difficult. It might sound silly, but all the messing around with the lion made me feel more like part of the group, so that when the day of the game came around, I was starting to feel like maybe I belonged in that team. Even if I knew I would have to earn my place.

I remember being on the bench for the Canada game and just repeatedly asking: 'Am I going on yet? Am I going on yet?' I must have driven the coaches and other players absolutely mad, but I was so impatient to get a chance to impress. As I waited, I kept going over so many things in my head – like, what happens when the coaches want you to go on? Do they call your name? What happens if I'm not ready to go on? What will happen if I miss a couple of tackles? I got a bit panicky to start with, but then, as I was sat there with my tracksuit on watching Jess score an incredible six tries on what was also her debut, I started to relax and I just said to myself: 'I'm going to have fun with this.'

I came on in the second half and scored a try, with Jess giving me a nice inside ball. It was the perfect way to mark a milestone game, which we won convincingly 79-5. Jess's double hat-trick made up a total of 13 England tries that day. At the moment I crossed the line, Jess jumped on top of me. We've got a photo of it and it's one I absolutely love. What's nice is that, since then, we've got plenty of similar photos from other games. I never jump on Jess. She always jumps on me. I think I'm a bit too tall – my feet would be scraping along the floor if I did the jumping. Before that first England camp, Jess and I weren't that close. But we've been great friends ever since.

That was a good moment, but I didn't really know what a full-back did. There were multiple times when the ball was kicked to me in the back field and I'd pick up possession and think: 'S***. I've no idea what I'm supposed to do here!' I didn't know whether to run or kick. Once, I tried booting the ball out into touch and it only went about 10 metres. It was absolute rubbish, because when you kick the ball, it should go way further than that. It's actually funny if you watch highlights of that Canada game back – the commentator says of me: 'She's meant to be the next Emily Scarratt.' That was quite the praise given Emily is an England rugby legend and one of the best backs to have ever played the game. Emily would go on to be a

CHAPTER 3

good friend of mine, but, at that point, I wasn't worthy of such a comparison.

When the game finished, I went to try and find my mum and dad in the crowd to celebrate winning my first cap. As I was looking for them, someone stopped me and said: 'Can I have a photo?' I said: 'Of course, no problem.' So, I took the phone and took a picture of the fans without me in it. It was only when they said, 'No, we want you in the picture' that I realised they wanted a selfie! I genuinely thought they just wanted me to take a photo of them. Then another person in the crowd said: 'Please can I have your autograph?' I didn't have an autograph to give them. I didn't know what mine was. At the time, I didn't even have a bank card let alone a proper signature. I had to make it up there and then and that autograph is still the one I use today – an 'E' for Ellie followed by a bit of a squiggle. Those incidents were very odd for a young girl who was still in college. I couldn't believe anyone would want a picture with me, or to collect my autograph. Then I saw my mum and dad. They were both hugely proud, obviously. But almost immediately my mum handed me my biology homework, and I had to run back across the pitch to the changing room with that in my hands.

Talk about being brought back to earth! The message from my mum was: 'Good game, but you've got some studying to do. Go on!' She's always been keen on putting education first. For my post-match song, a tradition for all international rugby debutants, I went with Bruno Mars.

That England camp involved a lot of growing up for me. It had to happen very quickly too. I was a second-year college student surrounded by women, some of whom were in their 30s, and many of whom had full-time jobs away from rugby. I didn't fully understand what the situation was with women's rugby at England level when I first joined the team. Unlike the country's top men's players, who had been paid to play since their game went professional in 1995, England women weren't contracted. But the Canada match in which I made my debut was not only hugely significant for me. It also had wider ramifications because, while there were still no full-time professional contracts, it was the first game in which the players from the England women's team were paid a match fee to play.

There was a lot of chat about the match fees coming in. The main talking point was how much we thought we should get paid. I had no idea what was going on. I was just rubbing my hands together as the prospect of receiving any money at all just for playing rugby was completely unfathomable to me, given I was still a college student. At the time I didn't realise that the investment was nowhere near what was required to make women's rugby successful, nor what the girls deserved, but I was buzzing. It was the first time I'd earned any money and I couldn't believe it. I was going to be rich! Unlike many of my teammates at that point, I had no responsibilities, so I used the money I received for my debut appearance against Canada – which was in the hundreds of pounds – to buy myself a pair of matte-black Beats headphones. They were very swish and when I went back to Gloucester-Hartpury a few weeks later I wore them in a running session. It's a bit embarrassing to admit now, but back then I thought I was the absolute s*** when I

CHAPTER 3

was wearing them. I was a college student who had gone and played for England at 18. Not only that, I now had some really cool headphones too. What I failed to realise was that the older girls were far more sensible and were either using the money we received to pay their employers back for lost time or to help pay off their mortgages. Their use of that historic first RFU payment was far more worthwhile than a pair of headphones because, at that point, players were either losing money or at best earning none at all from playing for England. It was very different then to the current situation, where we have contracts. It was all part of me learning a lot in a short space of time on the field, as well as growing up off it.

What did hit home, however, was that I had a real avenue to pursue. England players were now being paid. It was the beginning of a bright new era for women's rugby and the first proper step to the realisation that playing for England could become a full-time job. It was a hugely positive move for women's rugby and one I was able to appreciate, even as the youngest member of the squad.

Another memory I have of that time was one half term when during the break from college I went on a camp with England at Bisham Abbey. I stayed in the England camp on my own. I asked Ella Wyrwas if she wanted to come and visit and she said yes, so I went to go and pick her up from London. At that point, I'd never been to London properly before. I'd been there for a holiday when I was about seven, but that was it. I'd certainly never driven there. Ella wanted me to pick her up from Stone X Stadium. I put that into my maps and set off, but somehow

I ended up outside Harrods. I thought to myself: 'Jesus Christ, how have I ended up here in the centre of London?' I didn't know what I'd done wrong and to this day I still can't explain how it happened. That was a big shock as I'd become used to driving in Gloucestershire and Yorkshire where the roads are ever so slightly less busy than central London ...

I eventually picked Ella up and we made the journey back to Bisham Abbey for the weekend. There, we had a team room with a Nintendo Wii in it. We spent a whole day making different characters of all the England coaching staff on the Wii. I created one of Midds, making sure to use the angriest face I could. I had his eyebrows pointing vertically down and everything. I did loads of other profiles too, thinking no one would ever see them. But then when everyone came back into camp, the coaches came up to me one by one and said things like: 'Is that how old I really look then?' I was like: 'What?' And they said: 'Did you really think we wouldn't see those characters?' My reaction was: 'S***. Sorry.'

Even in my second year at Hartpury, after I'd been brought into the England squad, I was playing for Gloucester-Hartpury on a Saturday and then driving home to Yorkshire and playing football for Farsley on a Sunday. You couldn't get away with doing something like that now. But at the time, I was just so young and naive. I loved my football, so I didn't want to give it up. I got busted for the Nintendo Wii joke, but I was just a kid having a bit of fun. I was still playing rugby with the same joy I'd had when doing it for Keighley and West Park. The only difference was the quality of the rugby. I started playing because

CHAPTER 3

I loved the sport and I saw no reason for that to change, even if I had now become an international.

After my international debut, I was also involved in the final two matches of England's autumn campaign, both of which were against Canada again. It capped a crazy two months. My rugby career had escalated so quickly I hadn't had time to really take it all in. There were consequences, though, and one of them was a concern. Being called up by England at that time – before professionalism kicked in – involved going away to a training camp for two weeks and then playing matches for two or three weeks. For the older members of the squad, that meant having to take time away from work. In my case, the result was missing large chunks of study time at Hartpury.

In order to try and make up for that, I had specific school tutoring while I was in camp with England, with the aim of ensuring I didn't fall too far behind. For example, when there was a team meal in the evenings, I'd stay behind and do my schoolwork. It was something I had to do while following my rugby dream. I'd promised my parents I wouldn't let playing rugby impact my college grades. I hadn't made that promise lightly, but at the same time combining full-time education with international rugby was very difficult. It's not like I didn't try. I was determined and wanted to work hard, though the unfortunate result of progressing to rugby's highest level was that I encountered problems with my education.

What I would say, though, is that they were not all my fault.

4
Teacher Trouble

I studied geography, physical education and biology for my A-levels at Hartpury. In my first year, there were no problems in the classroom. But in the second, when I was first picked by England, I started to struggle to stay up to date, even with the help of the tutor while I was in camp. Because I'd be away from college I had to have a system where I'd be given all my classroom work in one- or two-week blocks, collected in this big binder, so I could take it with me wherever I went. Whenever I received a new binder, I would hand in the previous one. I found it all incredibly difficult. I might have had the odd telling-off at East Morton and Woodhouse Grove, but I massively enjoyed my time at both primary and secondary school. The reason for that, I believe, is because I work best when I really connect with the person who's teaching me. That could be in the classroom or on the rugby field. I thrive when I can make a personal connection with people, but because I wasn't at Hartpury very often in person during my second year, I couldn't build that.

I think it's so important for teachers and pupils or coaches and players to connect on a personal level, because it can really

CHAPTER 4

damage confidence if there isn't that bond or mutual respect. I can say that because it happened to me at Hartpury.

I had real problems with my A-level biology teacher. We had a difficult relationship. The teacher wasn't happy that I was missing lessons for rugby and that therefore when I was there in person, I didn't always know what was going on. I remember one particular biology class when I simply could not understand the lesson that was being taught. I'd done the work for it in my book, but because I had been away and not heard it all explained verbally, I just couldn't get my head around it all. I desperately flicked through my binder to check if I'd done the right work or not because I had none of the answers to the exercises I'd been set. I turned to the girl next to me and said: 'I think I've either done the wrong book here or don't have the right one.' And then I put my hand up to try and let the teacher know I was struggling. They responded: 'Ellie, I'm not talking now. I'm teaching.' I think they thought I was just making trouble, but all I was trying to do was communicate that I thought something was wrong. 'I'm not talking to you now, Ellie. Put your hand down,' the teacher said. I didn't know what to do. All I could think was 'S***. I'm going to England camp tomorrow and if I don't get this work done, I'm in trouble.' This was the only chance I had to get some in-person teaching before leaving again. It seemed clear to me I didn't have the right booklet, which wasn't my fault, but in response the teacher kept saying that I was distracting the class.

That wasn't true. I was just trying to draw their attention to the issue, so I then said out loud: 'I think I've got the wrong booklet.' The teacher lost it with me, shouting and screaming. They said I had problems and I needed to go get myself checked out. They said that something wasn't right with me in the head and, worst of all, that they thought I might be disabled. I stayed so quiet through all this, because I knew I couldn't fight back. Hartpury were helping me a great deal. There were lots of pupils playing high-level sport and studying for a BTEC, but I was the only A-level student studying at the college while also playing elite sport, and the system didn't really cater for that.

I might have appeared calm during this exchange, but below the surface I found it so, so stressful. All the time during that second year I was trying to balance the importance of a good education with more and more rugby commitments. I was so worried about my routine that, at the start of each day, I used to tear out a piece of paper from my notepad and write down every single moment of the day from the second I woke up. That included everything I did in terms of education and rugby, as well as my mealtimes and what I ate. My alarm went off at eight. My mum would call me by quarter past eight and we'd do half an hour of revision for my three A-level subjects. Then I'd go to breakfast at quarter to nine.

I kept the piece of paper in my pocket, and if the timings of my routine altered and ended up being different to what I'd written down, it would have a big impact on me. I'd have to write the whole schedule again from scratch. If a teacher was even a couple of minutes late to a meeting, that would worry me. It might mean I'd have to push other things back, and that might mean I wouldn't be able to sit down for lunch and instead

CHAPTER 4

I'd have to snatch a meal on the go, which in turn might impact my gym work later in the day.

I was just so overwhelmed with how busy I was, and the troubles in biology only made things way, way worse. I didn't know how to deal with it. This meant that in that moment when the teacher was trying to silence me, I was worried that if I fought back it would adversely affect my routine even further. So, I just nodded my head. But when the teacher said they thought I might be disabled, it left me feeling crushed inside. That comment really affected me and shattered my confidence.

The conversation ended with the teacher saying they were going to see the head of A-levels. I said: 'Fine, I'll see you down there.' We both went into the meeting straight away and sat down in a room separate from the main classroom. The teacher called me a bully and a distraction and said that because I was a female rugby player, other students were intimidated by me. It was absolutely crazy – all this commotion taking place just because I had tried to check if I'd got the right workbook. I cried my eyes out. I wanted to do well, as I always had done with my studies. I was trying my hardest. I was just helpless. It was teacher versus student. Who is the head of A-levels going to believe? Another teacher, who is their colleague, or a student? Why would a teacher lie about a student? I couldn't believe what was happening.

We came up with two options. One was that I could go to a different class and take the other A-level biology option. Every bone in my body wanted to do that, but I also knew I couldn't because it was a different syllabus and moving would mean I'd essentially have to start my studies all over again. The other was to carry on where I was.

I was the pupil. And they were the teacher. It wasn't a situation that helped me improve my work at all and my grades started to deteriorate as a result. I thought to myself: 'This is too much now. I can't do this.' And so, for the first time in my life, I pretty much gave up trying in all subjects, but especially biology. I didn't see how I could do all the work I had successfully, not with all the stresses of my daily college routine as well as rugby with England. I didn't say anything about it to anyone else for ages. That was my mistake. Talking about any struggles you might be experiencing – whether they are at school or in any other walk of life – is the best way to start combating them.

One day, I eventually opened up to my mum. The impact of the teacher's treatment on me was so severe that I pretty much broke down. My mum drove down to Hartpury instantly. She was there within hours and put the teacher straight. I believe that the biology teacher got sacked almost straight away. I haven't discussed that incident in detail with my mum since it happened, but I'm sure it was extremely difficult for her to hear about. Part of me hadn't wanted to tell my parents because I wanted them to think I was doing well. It was a big sacrifice for them to have their daughter move hundreds of miles away from home so young, and the last thing they would have wanted was to hear about the sort of trouble I had in biology.

Classroom drama only made me enjoy my rugby even more, something I didn't think was possible! Training and playing for Gloucester-Hartpury and England was the escape

CHAPTER 4

I needed. It was an interesting contrast, because at the start of 2018, and on the back of my England debut, I was selected for my first Six Nations. At that stage, the crowd numbers for the women's Championship games were growing quite slowly. But even if the attendances weren't huge, that Six Nations was a far bigger competition than the previous autumn campaign I'd been involved in. The matches were far more important and there were far bigger rivalries at play. I'd had three games at the end of 2017 to get a taste for international rugby. When the Six Nations began, I scored a late try in our 42-7 win over Italy in round one and then two in a 52-0 victory over Wales at The Stoop, but I was far from a certain starter and often on the bench. One of those Welsh scores was quite a nice one and I think that was the first time I really made a proper impact on an international game. I was starting to get more used to playing full-back and the requirements of the position. I grabbed my fourth try of the Six Nations in a 43-8 downing of Scotland in Glasgow that set up a round-four game with France in Grenoble.

Ahead of that game, Amy Cokayne – who I hadn't spoken to much up until that point – came up to me. Amy is our hooker and was already an experienced player. In my first Six Nations and with just a handful of caps, I was at the other end of the spectrum in terms of international knowhow. 'This is going to be different,' Amy said to me, referring to the challenge of facing France away. 'What's the biggest crowd you've ever played in front of?' I told her it was the Wales game at The Stoop. 'Prepare yourself,' Amy said.

I couldn't believe it when I walked out to check the pitch in Grenoble and saw how many people there were. The Beats headphones I'd bought were supposed to be noise cancelling, but I could still hear the French crowd through them. It was crazy – just so, so loud. In the last year or two, I've been fortunate to play in front of huge, huge crowds. But at the time, the 17,440 spectators in attendance for that Grenoble game felt absolutely massive to me. It was a new world record for a women's Test, breaking the previous best of 17,115 that had watched the 2017 World Cup final in Belfast between England and New Zealand.

The French were so noisy with their singing, chanting and banging of their drums. Everything about the match – both in terms of the quality of the rugby and the atmosphere – was on a different level to anything else I'd ever experienced. We had a great start, silencing the crowd with an early try from Abby Dow. But backed by some amazing support, France hit back with tries from Jessy Trémoulière and then Caroline Drouin to lead 10-7 at the break. Amy scored in the second half and after Katy Daley-McLean and Trémoulière exchanged penalties, we were 17-13 up heading into the final stages. But with just two minutes to go, Trémoulière scored the winning try.

It was my first loss as an England player and that game remains one of only two defeats I've suffered in a white shirt when playing 15s rugby. I'll always remember it, predominantly because I learned so much from it. I hadn't been a part of the previous World Cup and I knew we had a young team. But that didn't dull the pain. Losing to France meant we couldn't win a Grand Slam. Everyone was so sad. Even when I was trying to find the post-match meal hours after the final whistle, I was still crying and crying.

When I got back to my room, which on that trip I was sharing with Sarah Bern, I was alone as Sarah had to do drug testing. I sat on my bed and carried on crying. On the flight home, I listened to the song 'From Now On' from *The Greatest Showman* on repeat. It's a great tune but I kept getting teary-eyed. What that France game showed me was not only how much I cared about my rugby, but also what it meant to the people around me. Losing as part of an England team really hit me. France away in 2018 was my first real experience in rugby of losing an important match and not being good enough, both individually and as a team. Up until that point, whether it had been with Keighley, West Park or Gloucester-Hartpury, I'd become used to winning. Of course I had experienced losing. But on the whole, I hadn't suffered the pain of defeat when it really mattered. The same applied to my football career. As much as those situations hurt, they're good for you. In my opinion, you learn more from your painful experiences than you do your successes, and that France game was a very good example of that. France went on to win a Grand Slam, rendering our 33-11 win over Ireland in Coventry in the final round irrelevant. There was huge disappointment, but I ended that Six Nations as joint-top try-scorer, with five, alongside Trémoulière. I knew that from then on in, I'd always want to continue playing for England. It felt like my international career had really taken off.

Back at Hartpury a few months later and it was time for my A-levels and a reality check. When I got my exam grades in the summer of 2018 I thought I'd been given my mock results by mistake. I hadn't worked at all hard for my mock exams and got poor marks as a result. After that I did really try to knuckle down, but I still got the same marks – C in geography, D in PE and an E in biology. I thought to myself: 'What the hell. How can I have done so badly?' But looking back, I'm not sure why I was surprised, because in the Hartpury exam room I'd flick through the A-level test books in front of me on the desk, page by page, and have no idea whatsoever about any of the answers.

Sometimes, I'd be in class and my throat would close up. I couldn't breathe. I'd get really itchy and prickly skin. Similar to the experiences I'd had at Woodhouse Grove, these were physical signs of the mental stress and fatigue I was feeling. On another occasion, I was in the gym at a time when my mum was visiting and just feeling completely overwhelmed and stressed out. It wasn't a good sensation at all. My time with England meant I was away from college a lot and, when I was there, I had really struggled to build a personal connection with my teachers. The clash with the biology teacher was an extreme example, but on the whole my final college year didn't go well. That's the bottom line.

5

Sevens Switch

The fact we'd been paid a match fee on my England 15-a-side debut was a huge stride forward for the women's game because prior to that, the funding wasn't in place for that to happen.

But another gigantic leap came at the end of my second year at college. I had left Hartpury with disappointing grades, but on the rugby side there was huge excitement.

In 2018, England handed out fully professional contracts to its women's players in both 15s and sevens rugby. It was a huge moment. The girls who had come before me with England had to balance representing their country in rugby alongside other employment, because the money in women's sport was either non-existent or certainly not enough to live on. But that changed almost overnight as a result of the efforts of the RFU and their then chief executive Steve Brown. I was offered both a sevens contract and a 15s contract and told I could only take one. I was still only 18 but had scored nine tries in eight games in my first full season with England at 15s. I loved sevens, but I hadn't played the shorter format at the highest level. There was a big decision to make.

CHAPTER 5

I remember talking to Scott Bemand, the attack coach with England's 15s team, during training and he asked me what I wanted for my future. My response was pretty direct. I said: 'I want to be the best player in the world.' In my first season with England, because I was young and naive, I kept asking the coaches why I wasn't starting. They'd say they needed players with a bit more experience and that used to drive me mad. My view was you only got experience from exposure to matches. I wanted to get experience through playing, not just from being on the edges of a team for a certain amount of time. I told Scott: 'I want to go to an Olympics and I want to go to a World Cup.'

In the end, I took up the option of the sevens contract – a decision that meant I stopped playing 15s for Gloucester-Hartpury. I'd always loved playing rugby's shorter format and it was actually the form of the game I knew best. I'd done well in 15s with England, but at that point I saw sevens as a stronger weapon in my armoury. I saw what playing for England in sevens involved, and when it came to my two long-term targets, the sevens contest at the 2020 Tokyo Olympics would arrive before the 2021 15-a-side World Cup in New Zealand. I was also attracted by the prospect of travelling the world playing rugby. In rugby sevens, the matches are played all over the globe.

Again, I just saw that as one big sleepover with the prospect of seeing the world thrown in. It was a hugely enticing opportunity. There were 17 of us in total with professional sevens contracts, in a squad coached by James Bailey. Emily Scarratt, Heather Fisher, Natasha 'Mo' Hunt, Abbie Brown and Claire

Allan were amongst the experienced members. The switch to full-time status also involved the team moving from Bisham Abbey to The Lensbury Hotel in Teddington, where we'd share the same facilities as the England men's sevens side. But, first, I had to find a university to go to.

My England sevens contract was enough to live on, so I didn't have to continue with my education. But university was something my parents pushed massively. They stressed that, while I had signed my first rugby contract, there was still no guarantee of a long-term career in professional sport. My parents have always seen education as something you have to have and, although I'd had my fair share of stress while studying at Hartpury, it was the right decision to try and find a university. The message I received from my parents at the time was: 'Make sure you get yourself a degree because you never know what's going to happen.'

The fact I didn't do very well in my A-levels meant my initial desire to go to Loughborough University and study sport was never going to be fulfilled. I didn't get anywhere near the grades I needed to do that. But when I got offered the sevens contract and realised I'd be based at The Lensbury, I looked at St Mary's University in Twickenham. It made total sense geographically because the two places are a five-minute car ride away from each other. St Mary's ended up giving me a scholarship to study sports and exercise science. I also had a lot of support from the university, who allowed me to spread my studies over a longer period because my rugby commitments meant I would again miss lots of lecture time.

CHAPTER 5

I lived with Jess and Holly in a little house in West Molesey, near Hampton Court. Playing sevens rugby for a job was something completely new to all three of us. We were young and having the time of our lives. I absolutely loved it, even though for most of those first two years with the sevens I was injured. I suffered really badly with shin splints in both legs. Shin splits are a common injury, but very frustrating. I experienced pain and tenderness in the shin bones of my lower legs. Maybe it was a result of skipping all those exercises in the gym when I was in college. But I think it was also down to making that step up to another level; the sevens involved a far greater amount of running. The rugby workload was so much higher than I'd been used to and my body wasn't ready for it. It had to develop a lot more to accommodate the stress of training better.

While I was in and out of training, we had lots of fun. You get so tight with the people that you play with in sevens because it's a small squad, and they were a really good group of girls. We only lived 15 minutes away and we'd get to The Lensbury between eight and nine in the morning, have some breakfast and then train. After lunch, we'd go to the pool and the gym and then go home. I completely took it for granted. On Thursday evenings, we'd go to the pub and do a quiz.

Although the whole squad of 17 would train in Teddington, only 12 would go to the match weekends, wherever they were in the world. I got my first sevens cap for England in Colorado, but my shin splints meant I missed a lot of tournaments. It was the first time in my career that I had been injured and I didn't really understand it. My shins hurt constantly, and it wasn't like I had an injury like a broken leg, with a specific timeframe for healing. I had to be patient and try and understand my body.

That period of my life taught me so, so much. There were loads of rules around everything to do with the injury. I normally try to break rules, to be honest, but I was determined to recover, so I did what I was told. I had a certain number of steps – both walking and running – I could do each day, and at the end of it I had to send that number to the doctor. I had one or other of my legs in a boot countless times. We used to play around with kinesiology tape, a stretchy elastic sports tape that supports muscles and joints and helps with injuries. One that we found worked quite well was called Helter Skelter, so I wrapped that all around my legs in a desperate attempt to try and be fit enough to play. Nothing was working.

Then we thought maybe the pain was to do with my bones being too cold. So, I had to wear long socks and go to the sauna before training, to warm them up. That didn't help either. When I was in the gym, I couldn't start training fully until I could lift a certain weight or generate a specific amount of force because I had to prove my body was strong enough not to break down before going into rugby. Everything I did was measured.

Even when I was on the pitch I would be monitored using a GPS tracker. I could be about to score a try, or the ball would just be coming to me, but if my GPS numbers had gone past the distance threshold I'd been given, I'd be told: 'Ellie – off the pitch. Now.' That used to drive me insane. All I wanted to do was play but my body wouldn't allow it. I'd stand on the sidelines

CHAPTER 5

and do keep-ups with a football, but that annoyed the coaches, so then I was given a white deckchair I had to sit on.

I'd got this idea of going to the Olympics into my head and it just wasn't happening for me. I'd signed my first rugby contract but I spent more time sitting on the side of the pitch or in the gym than actually training. I'm impatient at the best of times, but at 18 I was climbing the walls with desperation.

I challenged myself to become better even if I couldn't train. I became really obsessed with watching training. I'd be there all the time, whether or not I was involved. I was learning things like the exact number of steps Helena Rowland, a fellow back, took before passing the ball. I wanted to work out how quickly she could catch and release, so I could time my runs next to her perfectly when I got back fit. I looked at the other teams we were playing. By the time we got to the Olympic qualifiers, I knew Russia inside out. I knew their centre preferred to step off her left foot when she caught the ball. I knew all the minute details I'd need to be successful on the pitch. The only problem – which was a pretty big one – was that I couldn't get on it.

At one point, I even spent two weeks in an intense rehabilitation unit (IRU). Not only had I been struggling with my shins, I'd also had shoulder surgery and my knees were starting to get sore as well. It was clear my body couldn't cope with the demands of professional rugby. The IRU was back at Bisham Abbey and it was very, very tough. I badly missed the camp environment with the girls back at The Lensbury. In my first week, I was there with a heptathlete called Niamh Emerson, who had problems with her hamstring. The aim for us both

Welcomed home after my birth on 8 September 1999 by my Granddad Ronnie, Grandma Julie and Granny Audrey.

With Granny Audrey in the garden of our first family home in Carr Lane, summer 2001. I don't remember Carr Lane as I was too young.

I've always been into cowboy hats! Alongside Holly Hellawell, daughter of Uncle Richard and Aunty Tracey, my godparents.

Banging out a rhythm on a drum set, aged three.

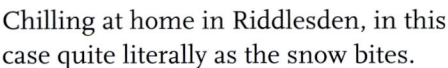

Chilling at home in Riddlesden, in this case quite literally as the snow bites.

My first job as a poster girl, in an advert for Bradford & Bingley Building Society, aged five. My mum worked in marketing there and it was where my creativity was first ignited.

I had a very active childhood. I'd play games like Cops & Robbers at home with my neighbours and always be on the go. This is me playing rounders with friends at Bolton Abbey.

My rugby journey started at Keighley Albion, which was a rugby league club. I first joined because my neighbours were going down there and I'd have had no-one to play with without them, so I followed suit!

I soon joined Keighly RUFC. I was the only girl in a team of boys.

Rugby wasn't my only love growing up. I was a huge Liverpool fan and big footballer. I started at Bingley Juniors and played alongside my rugby. Muddy weekend matches in both sports were a regular part of my childhood!

Getting stuck in at Keighley RUFC. The boys said they weren't tackling me because I was a girl. I knew the truth was different!

Earning my place in Woodhouse Grove's rugby first team after I was initially told to focus on other sports like netball! I'm centre of the front row as we celebrate a tournament win.

My parents worked hard so we were lucky to enjoy family holidays abroad. Larking around in the pool with my brother in Egypt.

Sam and I were very close in our early years and that remains the case today. I'm not really sure how to explain this picture … we'd get up to all sorts at home!

With Alfie, our family's border terrier, at the age of 13. We had lots and lots of animals growing up.

I was never the biggest and surrounded by boys, it would have been easy to give up rugby. But my love for the game meant that was never going to happen.

There is nothing like the sport of rugby for instilling values like teamwork. I learned that from a young age and it's still true today.

I've always been a proud Yorkshire girl. Representing the 'white rose' at regional level age 14.

My football career continued with Farsley Juniors, a team I won the national Under-16 Championships with. I was offered trials with Bradford City, but they wanted me to give up rugby which wasn't an option.

My 16th birthday party, surrounded by friends and family at home in Riddlesden.

I loved school at Woodhouse Grove and did well in my GCSE's but that didn't stop me burning my books when the exams were done!

I don't actually like heights, but I've always been a bit of a thrill seeker and love a new challenge. Cliff jumping on holiday in Carvoeiro, Portugal.

Turning 18 back at home in Yorkshire with my closest friends. I'd left home at 16 to join Hartpury College and progress my rugby.

Eventually playing alongside girls helped show me there was a path to playing women's rugby. Here I am with a National Sevens title, aged 15.

With John Normington, who was one of my first coaches at Keighley Albion. We're still close today.

Playing divisional rugby for Yorkshire and then North of England meant lots of travelling all around the country… and getting sleep as and when I could!

I was called up to England's senior training squad for the first time while still at school at Hartpury. My selection was a total shock.

I was 18 when I first appeared for England, but that didn't stop me from wanting to become a key figure in the team straight away.

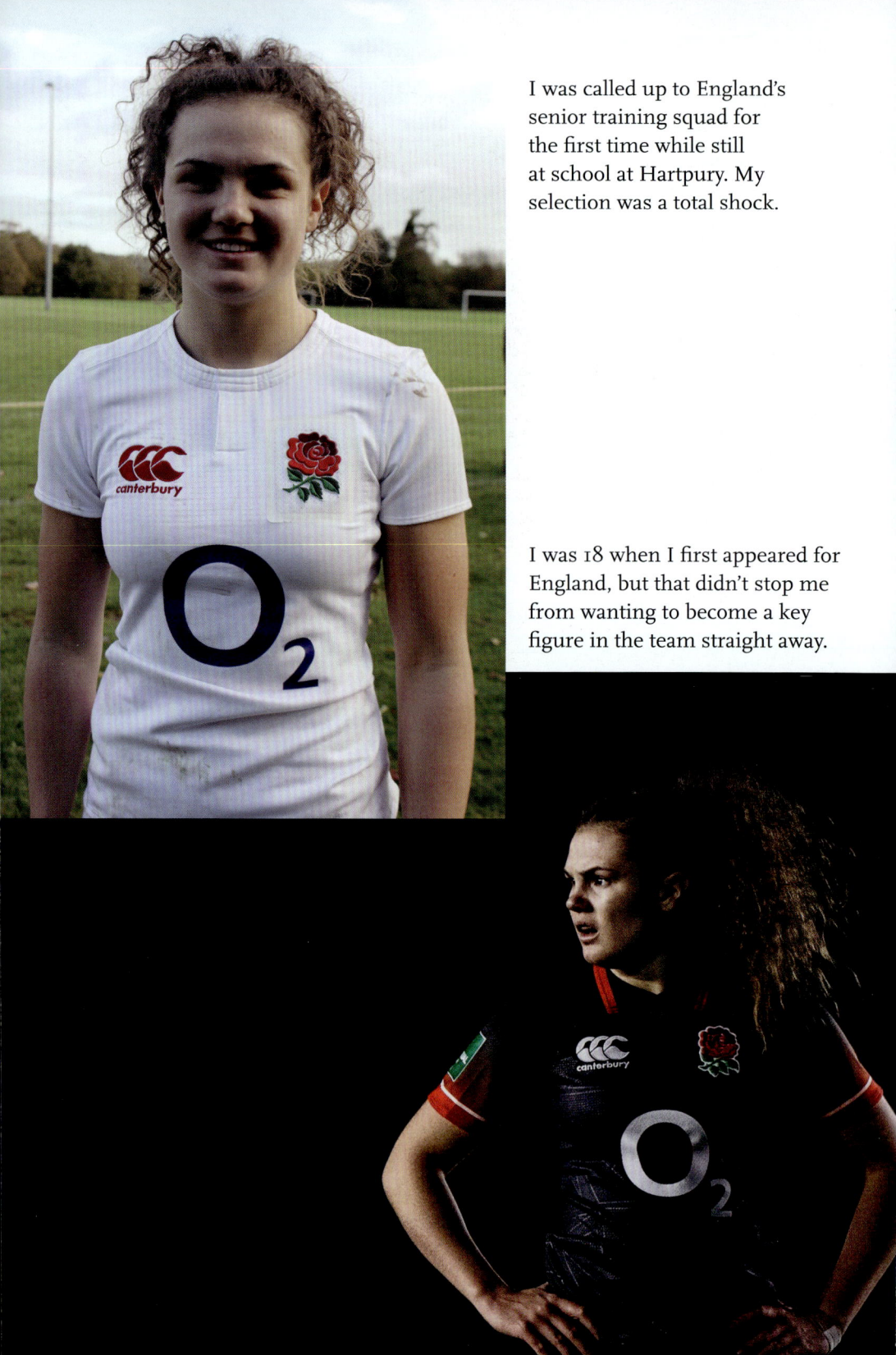

was to get back to fitness as quickly as possible. I'd wear a monitor on my chest 24/7, unless I was having a shower, to check my heart rate. Every morning, I would have to provide a blood sample from my ear. The aim was to increase my pain threshold, all with a view to me getting back fit enough to play. What we were put through was intense. There was one test where I'd push on a machine with my leg to measure the amount of force I could put through it. I'd have a cuff on my shin and the medics would send a force right through it, until it became too painful and I couldn't stand it any more. If I couldn't withstand a certain amount of force, it showed my body wasn't ready to play. The other thing they did was needling. It was like acupuncture, but so, so painful. With normal acupuncture, you put a needle into the body and leave it in so the muscles react around it. What we did for my shins was put a needle into my skin and then move it up and down and in and out of the skin. On the side of your shin bones, you have something called fascia, which is essentially soft tissue, and the needles would scrape along it with the aim of releasing pressure. Again, that was to try and get me used to pain. That was a really horrible experience.

When I started my second week at the IRU, Niamh had left and in her place was Chris Froome, the legendary British cyclist and four-time Tour de France winner. At the time, I was told not to say anything about him being there because people thought he was still in training, and he didn't want it made public that he was injured. I didn't know what was wrong with Froome but it was just me and him in the IRU. When I first saw him there I couldn't believe someone like me was sharing the same sporting facility with a sports star of his calibre.

One day that week we were both on exercise bikes together. Even though I was injured, I was asked to try and get my maximum power measurement on the static machine. I only cycled for 5 or 10 seconds, but I went like the clappers trying to hit the highest mark I could. When I was finished, Froome got on the bike next to me and with one leg produced four times the amount of power output I had with two. I couldn't believe it.

Froome is not a guy with noticeably big build, so his output was very impressive. In my naivety, I told him about all the different things we do in rugby training and in the gym, and asked him: 'Do you not get bored just cycling all the time?' I hated being on the bike myself. He told me he lived in France and would cycle stupid amounts of miles to get fit for big races. His attitude to training blew my mind and was a great lesson for me when I finally returned to the sevens.

By the summer of 2019, with the help of the time spent at the IRU alongside Froome, I was back to full fitness. As an England sevens team, our challenge was to try and qualify for the Tokyo Olympics, which were scheduled to take place in 2020. Because our World Rugby Sevens Series ranking wasn't good enough for automatic Olympic qualification, we had to go to Kazan in Russia for the next stage of qualification. I'd just returned to the pitch and apart from a competition in Marcoussis, France, I hadn't played any rugby at all before we got to Russia. We hadn't done well in Marcoussis, something that increased the pressure ahead of Russia. We knew that only by finishing first would we guarantee Olympic qualification. If we finished second, we'd then have to play another round of qualification matches – something we really wanted to avoid at all costs. We also knew we were in for a tough ride because our opponents – France, Ireland and Russia – were all teams we'd struggled against in the world series. Nevertheless, I was excited to play, because it was the first tournament at which I was deemed fit enough not to have my match minutes managed by the coaches. I was back firing on all cylinders.

The whole Russian experience was totally wild. When we arrived in Kazan, which is in the middle of Russia and an eight-hour drive from Moscow, the hotel gave us rooms with just one bed in them. But we were supposed to be sharing rooms, with two people in each. It was an obvious tactic to try and mess with our heads and ruin our preparation for the matches.

We had to think on our feet and ask the hotel to make more beds up. Some of the girls slept on sofa beds and some even shared a bed. The food was awful, too – not what we were used to at all. When we were doing our warm-ups and training on an indoor pitch, we found a camera that was secretly recording us. We weren't entirely sure who had put it there, but it was clear someone was trying to spy on us to find out our moves and gain a tactical advantage. It was crazy. I'd never experienced anything like it before.

We didn't let the distractions get to us and, if anything, the attempts to derail our performance only served to spur us on more. During the pool stage we beat Ireland and France, before losing to Russia 26-5. Then, in the final, we were once again

CHAPTER 5

matched against Russia, who had the benefit of home advantage. Just before kick-off, the organisers opened up the stadium gates, so the place was absolutely filled with Russia fans. It felt like the whole world was against us, except for my mum and her friend, who were the only England fans to have come over. After all, the tournament was in deepest, darkest Russia, not an easy trip.

Beating Russia in the final was particularly sweet for a number of reasons. We'd come through all sorts of issues to win the tournament, turning the tables on the hosts in the final – a fantastic moment. It meant England had secured Olympic qualification. Being a part of the squad in Russia was also special to me given the tough years I'd had with injury. Tokyo 2020 was now in all our sights, but what happened next was something no one could have foreseen coming.

The Covid-19 pandemic not only turned the whole world upside down; it also changed the direction of my rugby career.

6
Rocky Road

It was in March of 2020 that the Japan Games suddenly started to feel very real.

After sealing qualification in Russia, all of a sudden we were just months away from the scheduled start of the Olympics. Our training was ramping up at The Lensbury as a result, with everyone – including me – bidding to earn selection. But then, after we'd finished one particularly gruelling session, the players were all called inside and told how serious Covid-19 had become. In the previous few weeks, like everyone else, I'd seen reports on the news of a virus spreading around the globe, originating in China. I was aware of what was happening, but never in a million years did I think it would impact me. So, when Boris Johnson – the prime minister at the time – appeared on television and informed the public that everyone would have to isolate at home to stop the spread of the disease, I was left totally shellshocked. Clearly, isolating at home meant rugby training was completely off the cards. It was quickly announced that the Japan Olympics would have to be delayed by a year. No one knew what would happen next.

CHAPTER 6

Initially, I went back home to Yorkshire to be with my family. There was a positive to that as it was the first time I'd been able to spend a significant period of time in Riddlesden since I'd left for Hartpury when I was 16. Nevertheless, like a lot of people, I found the Covid period very tough. I think the reason it had an especially big impact on me was because I went from the team environment of the England sevens to being on my own for long periods. I was now unable to train with my teammates, which was difficult in itself, but I still had to try and stay fit. I'd gone from preparing for an Olympics to having nothing on the horizon, so I also needed something to fuel my competitive drive. To do that, I started going on daily five-kilometre runs. I quickly became very fixated on them. Just as quickly, what should have been a healthy habit became an unhealthy obsession. I thought I was helping myself by staying fit, but in other ways I was doing damage.

I became determined to set a new personal best each time I did a run. Clearly, that was unrealistic. I'd drive around – once the rules about isolation were relaxed enough to allow that – to try and find the terrain or running route that would give me the best chance of setting a new record. At night, I couldn't go to sleep because I was trying to work out the split times I'd have to run for each kilometre in order to beat my previous best. On some runs, I'd realise halfway I wasn't going to set a new record, so I would give up and walk back to my car because I didn't see the point in completing the run. It was a new record or nothing. On some days, I'd run in the morning and at night. Part of that was down to boredom, because I had nothing else to do, but I was also addicted to it. I'm a person that tends to hyper-focus on something once I've set my mind on it. I have a very obsessive nature and an addictive personality. Alongside the running, I also damaged myself with the way I ate. I lost lots and lots of weight during that time. I didn't have a good relationship with food at all.

I remember being at the house of one of my sevens teammates in Twickenham once I was back in London, after Covid-19 restrictions had been lifted a little to allow some socialising. They said they'd cooked food for me and that it would be ready in half an hour. We were watching television, but as soon as they'd spoken I jumped up and told everyone I was going out for a run. I didn't warm up or stretch. I just went out and ran because I felt like I needed to earn the food I was about to eat. I knew how many calories were in everything I ate – even down to a piece of bread. I knew how many calories a female athlete needs to consume on a daily basis, but I'd try and get under that number. I just became super obsessed with getting smaller. I used to do regular body checks by taking pictures of myself with my arms in the air. It wasn't to check if I was getting stronger. I wanted to check to see if I was getting smaller.

It all started with running. In my head, I believed that I'd be quicker at running if I was smaller and skinnier. It was a damaging mindset, but that's how I thought at the time. I know many other people have experienced similar problems.

The five-kilometre run times were all about competitiveness, and then the eagerness to get better at that started to affect what I ate and when, and the way my body looked as well. It was about wanting to have control over how I looked. That was what I was chasing. I wanted to be the player that was small.

The problems with my diet were more prevalent when I was in London. I did spend a fair amount of time in Yorkshire at the start of the pandemic in order to be with my family. I was more restrained when I was there, because I didn't want my mum and dad to find out about what I was going through. Still, it quickly became a big, big issue in my life. It used to upset me when I'd eat food, especially if it was something I saw as unhealthy. I went through a phase of eating nothing but salads. On one occasion, I was with my mum and dad and they said to me: 'Shall we go out for a burger?' I would normally have been really excited by that, because I love burgers. But, at that time, the thought of eating a burger would make me really anxious. I was thinking: 'If I eat a burger, it's not going to make me smaller and it's not going to make me faster. If anything, it's going to make me bigger and slower and that's not what I want.' That's why I'd get upset and would stick only to salad. That's not a healthy way of living, but I thought it would help me get to where I wanted to be.

I just couldn't stop the thoughts controlling my eating. I'm quite small anyway, but I had crippling body dysmorphia that impacted me both mentally and physically. I felt like I was really fighting against the odds in all aspects of my life.

Covid-19's impact was not just personal to me. Far from it, in fact. The results were calamitous, many people losing their lives. The economy was devastated, and in rugby the ramifications were huge too. Clubs in both the men's and women's game were left in financial trouble as a result of not being able to play matches. When rugby was allowed to return, social distancing meant there could be no crowds. Clubs and national unions therefore couldn't generate money, leaving the RFU with some tough decisions to make. At the time, the RFU was budgeting for an expected loss of £107 million because of Covid. The brutal result was that in order to reduce costs and stay financially stable as a business, in July 2020 the RFU cut its funding to the England sevens programmes, for both men and women. We were told in a conference call that there wasn't the money to keep the team going. England's women's sevens team folded on the spot, with the players all instantly made redundant.

Losing my job through no fault of my own could well have been the end of my rugby career. Like everyone in the world at that time, I was dealing with an element of the unknown.

After we were told that we were no longer contracted to the sevens, I didn't know what the next day looked like, let alone my long-term future. But I didn't worry. Even with everything that was going on at the time, I still knew I wanted to become the best rugby player in the world. I remained confident I'd find a way to do that.

Like anyone who lost their job in the Covid years, I was forced to look for other work. I explored the option of nannying and bar jobs in the Twickenham area, while I also remained enrolled at St Mary's University. It was something I didn't want to do, but I had no other choice. Fortunately, while the sevens had come to an end, 15s rugby eventually began to return and, alongside several of my former sevens teammates, I signed a

CHAPTER 6

deal with Wasps, whose women's team was based in Ealing, not too far from where we'd been training in Teddington. Wasps offered me a rugby lifeline at a time when I didn't have another option. It was a crucial turning point, but I still hadn't got my eating under control.

I walked into the gym at Wasps one day and someone remarked: 'God, Ellie. You need to eat a burger.' I thought to myself: 'Next time you see me, I'm going to be even smaller.' You simply can't have that sort of mindset and expect to be successful as a professional athlete. But that's where I was at the time.

On another occasion, the England physio Emily Ross came down to a Wasps session. I'd worked with Emily with the sevens, but she had moved back to the 15s after it had folded.

Emily sat me down and was very honest with me. She could do that because we knew each other so well.

'Ellie, you're really small at the moment,' she said. Is everything okay?' I burst into tears. Up until Emily had asked me that question, I'd hid my issues with food from everyone. My parents remained completely unaware of what I'd been going through for the past six months. Crying to Emily was the first time I'd engaged with anyone on the topic or showed any emotion. I was exhausted. I just didn't have any energy left because I wasn't fuelling my body properly.

When I look back on that period now, I don't have a f****** clue why I did it. It totally blows my mind, because if any of my friends came to me now and told me they were doing the same thing, I'd go absolutely mad at them. But the truth is, that is what I did at the time. It was self-sabotage – pure and simple.

I'm very aware that I'm not the only young person who has experienced issues with food, their weight and body dysmorphia. I think talking about what you're going through with others is a huge thing, whether it's to your parents, friends or someone else you feel you can trust. I was never going to come out of that downward spiral by trying to deal with everything myself. And if you can't help yourself, then nor will anybody else, unless you tell them what you are going through.

If a person puts weight on, it's seen as unhealthy and a negative thing. But when you lose weight, it's seen in society as a positive. You get compliments for it. You would never go up to someone who has gained weight and say: 'God, you need to lay off the burgers.' Clearly, that is really going to offend that person. But people see it as a compliment to be told they are looking thinner. It certainly didn't make me upset. If someone said to me that I looked small, I'd take it as a challenge. 'Just you wait,' I'd be thinking, 'I'll be even smaller tomorrow. I won't eat anything until then.' I'm always so careful now of what I say around someone who has either gained or lost weight, because that could only be half their story. On the face of things, I probably looked fit and healthy for much of Covid-19, as I was running a lot. But the reality was very, very different.

Talking about what I was going through with Emily – as much as it was difficult – gave me accountability and got me back on track. I would urge anyone who is now, or has been, in the same position as me to realise that your body is a tool and has been put on this earth to do amazing things. If you're struggling with negative thoughts around your weight or appearance,

CHAPTER 6

it helps to see food as fuel. I had times in the pandemic where I hated eating. That was so sad because I love food. Now I see it as something I need to make me who I am today as a rugby player. But it doesn't matter what you do in life. Whoever you are, food is fuel.

I chose to fight my battles with food on my own. I didn't have to and should have sought help sooner. But I am now a more resilient and stronger person for the experiences I've gone through. I've had to learn how to get myself out of a rut when my whole body is telling me to stay in it.

It was at this point, when I'd just started with Wasps but was still not totally sure of my next step, that I got a call from the England 15-a-side coach Simon Middleton. I was told there was the option of a full England contract in 15s, which would have offered financial and sporting stability. But, if I took it, I would not be allowed to go to the Japan Olympics. It was an incredibly tough position to be in. On the one hand, I desperately wanted to represent my country at the Tokyo Games, even though as players we were unsure of what that would look like after the England team was disbanded. The prospect of moving away from sevens in an Olympics year felt tantamount to torture, not only because of my own personal desire to compete in what is widely seen as sport's pinnacle, but also because I had a huge amount of love for my team. We'd gone through a tough couple of years together, most of which I'd spent on the sidelines. As I've said, a sevens squad is very different to 15s – much closer knit. We were really, really tight and I didn't want to leave them behind. More than just teammates, I counted them all as friends.

But I'd also realised that having struggled so badly with shin splints for the best part of two years, standing on my feet while working a day job alongside trying to play sevens part time, wasn't going to put me on course to become the best player in the world. I agonised about which option I should take for weeks, sitting alone in my car for long periods and worrying about the repercussions of my decision. I couldn't help but feel I was throwing away my dream. But, eventually, I signed the 15-a-side deal. I felt a lot of guilt and shame about doing so because even though I'd spent a long period of time with the sevens injured, I still felt a really close connection to the squad. We'd spent so much time together. I loved the group. I also didn't want other players to see my decision as a cop-out, because some of the girls did take on nannying jobs and bar work to help support their rugby. When I finally made my decision, I called every single person in the team – staff and players – and spoke to them to explain. A WhatsApp message on a group chat would not have been enough. I explained to them why I was making my decision. I said I wanted to be the best player in the world and that I didn't believe that working two jobs – even though other girls were doing it – was the right path for me to get to that goal.

Opening up to Emily about my eating was a defining moment for me. It was the first step to getting back on track, but the weight loss, unsurprisingly, affected my rugby. When Covid-19 started to relent and the world opened up a little, we got back into full training and matches with Wasps. I'd signed for them in September 2020, but the games didn't really get up and running until 2021. I didn't play well.

CHAPTER 6

I'd damaged my body and that took a while to recover from. And it took longer than I'd hoped to successfully adapt back to 15s rugby. It wasn't anything to do with the sport as such. It was because I was too skinny.

I was scoring lots of tries with Wasps because, when I got the ball in space, I still had the speed to escape other players and make it to the line. But in the physical confrontations, I'd lose the ball when I'd go into contact. Other players would just rip it off me easily – I didn't have the strength and physicality needed to compete with other professionals. I also lost my confidence in tackling, knowing my weight loss meant I was more likely to get injured. I wasn't playing anywhere near my best at club level, and that impacted on the prospects of my return to the England team. There was no way I was going to be selected to start at international level if my poor performances with Wasps persisted.

I remember crying a lot through that period. And, I mean, a lot. I'd had struggles with my weight, had to make a huge decision to step away from the Olympics – which had been a dream of mine – and now I wasn't playing well in 15s. I had a big challenge to get back to my best.

Being an international athlete is tough enough in normal circumstances. Professional rugby is very demanding on your body. But my weight loss meant I just wasn't equipped to cope with it. I soon got injured. I was called back into an England camp to train, and very quickly suffered a stress fracture in my knee. When I went for the medical checks to assess the damage, I had bone density tests as well as blood tests. My bone density was found to be good, so it was quite clear I'd suffered the injury because I didn't have enough muscle on me. It opened my eyes to the realities of what I'd done to myself.

Things had to change there and then because I wasn't prepared to suffer any further rugby setbacks. Although I've always been one of the smaller players on the field, I've also prided myself on being brave and physical in the contact. Getting smashed every two seconds and losing the ball was just not me. Having seen food as something I wanted to avoid throughout the pandemic, the knee injury totally switched my mindset and, slowly, I started to get back on track.

Like everything else, the 2020 Six Nations was impacted by the pandemic, with some of its matches postponed to later in the year. On 1 November, after recovering from the injury and incrementally returning to somewhere near my best, I was back in an England shirt for a 54-0 win over Italy in Parma. The Championship had already been secured in the months before, but starting against the Azzurri presented me with a big chance to remind the coaching staff of my ability. I scored the opening try in just the fourth minute, as the team claimed a second consecutive Grand Slam. Because I'd only just returned to the 15s side, I didn't really feel a full part of the success. But at the same time, after all my struggles, it was nice to be back winning on the field.

After just one season at Wasps, I decided I needed a change and signed for Harlequins. I was seen as quite difficult at Wasps and that was a perception I struggled to change. I was often late for training, and I challenged the coach Giselle Mather regularly.

CHAPTER 6

I love Giselle and we really get on now. But I'd get quite frustrated during training and, when I felt the time was right, I would air my thoughts about what I thought we were doing wrong.

I was still living at the house in West Molesey with the sevens girls at that time. But I was also often staying overnight in Reading at Cameron Sommerville-Bailey's mum's house. Cam's brother James Bailey had coached me with England sevens. I'd met him once or twice before that, but that was our mutual connection. Having started a relationship with Cam, the change in my personal life was accompanied by a feeling that it was time to think about changing other aspects of my everyday existence.

The diet issues I'd had weren't helped by the amount of travelling I was doing between two houses and travelling to training. I was basically living out of my car due to being on the road all the time. I'd be eating on the go, often grabbing meal deals from a supermarket for convenience. I knew that for my own good this had to change. And so, signing a deal with Harlequins and buying my first house in Reading, where Cam was from, was the right combination at the right time. I bought the house on my own, a decision that was motivated by the thought that it would be good to invest some of my money into property. Losing my job with the sevens had scared me – all the security I had was taken away from me in an instant. I wanted to make sure I had some solid foundations.

I was fortunate that my sponsor at the time was Canterbury, and they paid my first year's salary in one lump sum. It gave me the funds to put down a deposit to buy a house. After a little while, Cam moved in with me. He was a great support. A video he put out in which he said he washed my boots went viral. Doing those sorts of things was his love language. I learned so much living with Cam. Professional athletes get a lot of attention for their achievements. But I don't think enough light gets shone on the partners of those sportsmen and women. It is very hard for them. In the time Cam and I had together, I'd often go away for weeks on end, and our training with Harlequins meant I'd get home late at night.

As well as washing my boots, Cam would cook and tidy the house. He would fold his clothes in a certain way and I'd do the same. He had a creative spark, like me. I've got so many fond memories of that house after we'd moved in together. I'll forever be grateful for the time we spent as a couple and, even though we're not together now, we remain in contact. I wouldn't be the player and person I am now without the part Cam played in my life.

In March 2021, it was announced that the 15-a-side World Cup in New Zealand – which had been planned for later that year – had been postponed until September 2022. Again, Covid-19 was the reason. We were in camp with England at the time and the sevens girls had joined us for training. I'll never forget Midds going around the group and saying that the World Cup delay would help the squad, as he'd be able to add some of the sevens girls back into the group. My heart sank when he said that, because it made me feel like I could have played in both tournaments. I had been told that wasn't possible, but in an ideal world that's what I'd have done. I'm a strong believer

CHAPTER 6

that everything happens for a reason, but I remember in that moment feeling an element of regret at the choices I'd made.

The 2021 Six Nations was pushed back from January to April, and the format of the Championship had to be changed. The competing countries were divided into two pools of three teams, meaning that not every side played each other. As a result, there was no Grand Slam that year.

I couldn't get into the starting 15 regularly because my performances were too inconsistent. The coaches at the time wanted me to play a version of the full-back role that in my opinion didn't suit my game. They wanted me to play like Freddie Steward, who is a brilliant No. 15 for the England men's team as well as Leicester Tigers, but also a completely different sort of player to me.

Steward is fantastic under the high ball and a good kicker, and I felt that the coaches had this idea in their heads that that's how a full-back should play. My strengths are very different – I can kick, but I'm much more of a runner. Although I enjoyed my time with the team, I don't think the coaches got the best out of me consistently during that period. They were quite hard on me with their messaging, making it clear how they wanted me to play, and why I wasn't being selected as a regular starter. I took their words on board, but deep down I didn't feel they were right.

I was on the bench against Scotland for the first pool game, started against Ireland, but was then back as a replacement for the final with France. As soon as we had a high-pressure game, I would be on the bench, at best. I was in and out, in and out, and I couldn't find my flow. I had a fear of failure, as well as a fear of not fitting into the mould of what the coaches wanted from their full-back. I don't think I was given a fair opportunity to show my worth.

Shaunagh Brown, our prop forward, was in a similar position to me at that time. Shaunagh was also not a regular starter and a bit frustrated as a result. One day, I was in Shaunagh's room and, to have a bit of fun and pass some time, we decided to compare each player in the squad to a different type of shoe. For example, we agreed that Emily Scarratt was like a Christian Louboutin heel because she was the queen of English rugby and just very, very classy. We went through the squad one by one. Shaunagh and I both said that we were like the leather boots of the England squad. Everyone has a pair of old leather boots. Every year, you tell yourself you're going to chuck them out because you've had them ages. But for whatever reason, you just can't because they're so comfortable. They do the job. They're always there when you need them. That's how Shaunagh and I felt at the time. We were players who were seen as reliable when needed but when the big games came, we were left out. I wanted that to change. It frustrated me greatly that I was a leather boot. I wanted to be a Christian Louboutin like Emily.

In the summer of 2021, I had to watch the Tokyo Olympics from afar. It had been a tough time for the England girls who had stayed with the sevens. The withdrawal of RFU funding had meant they'd worked part-time jobs and with money tight due to the impact of Covid-19, England had joined forces with Wales and Scotland to come together as one team. As a combined team they were competing under a Great British banner. The 13-player

CHAPTER 6

squad was packed full of players I'd been training with consistently for the previous two years – the likes of Holly Aitchison, Mo Hunt, Megan Jones and Helena Rowland. It was completed by Wales's Jasmine Joyce, and Hannah Smith and Lisa Thomson from Scotland. I thought I would find it hard to watch the team play, given the time I'd spent with them in the build-up and the fact I was no longer there. There was still a tiny bit of envy at my former teammates experiencing an Olympics without me, but that was completely overridden by my desire for the team do well. I'd already accepted that I wasn't able to go to Tokyo and it's never difficult to watch your friends be successful. In life, you have to accept the choices you make, and I had made peace with my decision to return to 15s. I also knew how good that Great Britain team could be, because I'd worked with them for so long.

I just wish they'd ended with a medal. To finish fourth was a fantastic effort, but to see the team lose the bronze medal match 21-12 to Fiji was hard to take. I think they deserved to be on that podium.

My focus had switched to a new long-term goal – the 15-a-side World Cup in New Zealand. The fact that tournament had also been delayed by a year gave me more time to return to my best and make more of an impression on the England squad. I had settled into life at Harlequins well and, looking back now, that time taught me a valuable lesson – one I didn't really appreciate at the time. I now know that the more I play, the better I play.

I'm a player who thrives on regular minutes, and while I was a squad regular by the time of the 2022 Six Nations, I was not always in the starting XV. That didn't change throughout that Championship. I did start the 57-5 and 74-0 victories over Scotland and Italy but was on the bench for the remaining three matches, with Abby Dow and then Helena Rowland beginning at No. 15 instead. I did have to come on early to replace Abby against Wales, but in the Grand Slam-sealing win away to France, I got just seven minutes off the bench. I got the impression that the coaches still weren't totally sure who they wanted at full-back. Being part of another Grand Slam was special, but on an individual level I knew I was still a leather boot. The journey to becoming a Christian Louboutin continued ...

7
Final Heartbreak

The England team travelled to the delayed World Cup in New Zealand in 2022 with real belief we could win the tournament. It was fuelled by the fact that we headed to the southern hemisphere on the back of an impressive 25-match winning run. England's last loss in 15s had been the 2018 Six Nations defeat by France in Grenoble, a game I'd been involved in and still had scars from. In the matches since that loss, I'd been away from the squad at points due to playing sevens. At others, I hadn't always been involved – not heavily anyway.

But when we arrived in New Zealand in late September, I still had a huge, huge sense of excitement at the prospect of playing at my first World Cup. I was 23 and, after struggling with injury while with the sevens, I felt the fittest and strongest I had ever been in my time as a professional. The problems I'd had with my eating were, thankfully, behind me. Having missed out on the Tokyo Olympics, the World Cup was undoubtedly the biggest tournament of my career so far. Rugby is everything to the people of New Zealand, something we realised as soon as we landed in Auckland. The World Cup was based in the country's North Island, in Auckland and Whangārei. Once we'd

CHAPTER 7

got the long flight out of our system and the opening ceremony was finished, I couldn't wait for the action to get going. I knew I was far from a certain starter, but my confidence was still high. I believed if I was given a chance, I'd be able to perform well. There was significant expectation on us to win.

Earlier that year, we'd seen England's women's footballers win the 2022 European Championship by beating Germany at Wembley thanks to Chloe Kelly's goal, followed by her iconic celebration. After watching the Lionesses lift that title, there was a sense among us rugby players that it was now our turn.

While on-field matters were our obvious focus, New Zealand also provided me with the chance to explore a truly wonderful country. I'd been fortunate enough to travel the world before that, as a child and then through playing rugby. But on the back of the pandemic, when you couldn't even leave your house at times, let alone fly to the other side of the globe, the opportunity to go to New Zealand was priceless. I felt lucky and grateful – well aware that the opportunity to travel to a country so far from home was something many people never experience in their lives. And here I was being paid to go there to play rugby in a World Cup.

For the majority of the tournament we were based for the whole tournament in Auckland, which is a fantastic city. In our downtime, I did a lot of shopping. I explored the city's thrift shops looking for vintage fashion, particularly in trendy areas of the city like Ponsonby. One of my favourite things to do was to hire scooters. We'd often go out on them in the evenings. We'd zoom about and stop off at a street food vendor to get some dumplings for a late-night snack. There is quite a big Japanese culture in Auckland, so the karaoke bars were also a popular haunt. There was one in particular, which we visited on several occasions, that had individual pods you could sit in and sing. I've always loved karaoke. We'd sing anything and everything, but one of my strongest memories is singing Beyoncé's 'Ave Maria' with Detysha Harper, who had been a late call-up to the squad.

Auckland's most iconic monument is the Sky Tower, which we also went up. Playing in a World Cup meant we were never going to bungee jump off it, which would otherwise be possible. We had to make do with watching others do that.

New Zealand is one of the most picturesque places I've ever been to. We'd travelled out early to acclimatise, but ahead of our first game we were told that if we wanted we could spend a night away from the designated team hotel. I was always going to take up that option and was one of a group who hired an amazing Airbnb. The setting was like something out of a James Bond film – stunning mountains set against calm lakes. That night was very relaxed and wholesome. We made some food, went in the jacuzzi and relaxed.

The next day, we'd planned to go down to the beach and to see some of New Zealand's famous waterfalls. When we're abroad with England, we always have a team liaison officer with us, a person from the area who can help us with anything we need. In New Zealand, our liaison officer was an English guy called Danny who had been living in the country for a long time. He offered to show us around, and first we headed down to a local beach. It was far from warm, but we jumped in the sea anyway. In fact, it was freezing. I hadn't expected it to be so cold.

CHAPTER 7

We got out, went back to the bus and everyone else put spare clothes on, before we headed off to see a waterfall. Being my usual self, I'd forgotten to bring anything to change into. By the time we'd arrived at Karekare Falls, I'd dried off, but it was so beautiful that we all egged each other on to jump into the water once again. The water was baltic and I nearly drowned trying to video myself getting under the waterfall. Then we had to walk two kilometres back to the bus. I was definitely on the verge of hypothermia. It had been fun while it lasted, but as I tried to descend the steps back to the car park, shaking with cold as I did so, I did wonder if it was the best preparation for a big tournament.

Our winning run meant we were one of the World Cup's top seeds, alongside hosts New Zealand and Canada. We had been drawn in Pool C, with Fiji, France and South Africa. I was particularly looking forward to facing Fiji and South Africa, who would be unfamiliar opponents. My experience of 15s rugby to that point had been my debut autumn series against Canada in 2017 and then regular matches with France, Wales, Italy, Scotland and Ireland in the Six Nations. Fiji and South Africa would present a new challenge. Equally, we were also keenly aware that being in the same pool as France was a very tough draw – they were not only the last team to beat us, but also our fiercest rivals in Europe.

Even though I started the 84-19 hammering of Fiji at Eden Park and the 13-7 victory over France in Whangārei, I still didn't feel a key figure within the team. The French victory was the most important, because that secured our progress to the knock-out stages. Emily Scarratt scored all our points that day, emphasising why she was and always will be a Christian Louboutin of English rugby. I'd been happy enough, but not delighted, with my performances in the Six Nations, and the same could be said of my World Cup starts against Fiji and France. Not bad. But could do better. I only played for a few minutes in the 75-0 win over South Africa, which rounded off the pool stages and set up a quarter-final with Australia.

When that game with the Wallaroos came around, I was on the bench, with Helena Rowland starting at full-back. Helena had been playing really well, both in the run-up to and at that World Cup, and I was well aware that Midds and the rest of the coaches had been very impressed by her performances. I could understand why. I'd played and trained with Helena for a long time by then, both in sevens and 15s, so knew what a phenomenal player she is. At the same time, I wasn't as consistent at that World Cup as I would have liked to have been. When we would sit down for the squad meetings where the team was announced, I'd have no idea what to expect: would I be starting, on the bench or not in the matchday squad at all? I don't think that uncertainty helped me, but I could also understand it, because I wasn't playing good enough rugby to be a nailed-on selection. I tried to control what I could control. I trained as hard and as well as possible, and when I was given the chance to play I did that to the best of my ability. Ultimately, that's all you can do as a player.

We beat Australia 41-5 at Waitakere Stadium in Auckland. It was a comfortable win played in horrific conditions. Driving

CHAPTER 7

rain meant the ball was like a bar of soap. It wasn't a game for running rugby, but our forwards stepped up, with Marlie Packer scoring a hat-trick.

Canada were our semi-final opponents and, given the way the World Cup had gone so far, I wasn't surprised to be on the bench. I was No. 23 again, with Helena now in possession of the No. 15 shirt. Just before that game, our prop Hannah Botterman and scrum-half Lucy Packer were forced by injury to withdraw. I watched from the bench as Helena created a fine try for Abby Dow. Abby had been on fire in the tournament after miraculously recovering from a broken leg that had cast significant doubt on her ability to even make the trip. She'd made an incredible comeback with the help of Emily Ross. Despite a bit of pre-match upheaval, some late replacements coming in and a strong Canadian performance, we had a 15-12 half-time lead.

My World Cup changed in a split second five minutes into the second half at Eden Park. Helena suffered a serious ankle injury and couldn't continue. You never, ever want to see a teammate get injured. Even though Helena and I were rivals for the same position, we were also very close, having been in the same squads in both sevens and 15s for a long time. It was immediately pretty clear that her problem was serious, but as Helena limped off I didn't have time to let emotion take over. I had a big job to do in a World Cup semi-final.

Just three minutes after I'd come on, we attacked from deep. When Zoe Harrison passed the ball to Claudia Moloney-MacDonald (née MacDonald), both players were in our dead ball area – right at our end of the pitch. Scoring a try from such a position is normally a nigh-on impossible task. It wasn't that day. Claudia weaved in and out of the black-shirted Canadian players and passed to Abby. I sprinted up alongside Abby in support but wasn't needed as she raced away to score one of the tries of the World Cup. We'd gone the length of the field in a matter of seconds, the try a crucial moment in sending us through to the final. The 26-19 win was our 30th successive victory. But it had also been by far our toughest test for more than a year. Canada had challenged us in ways other teams hadn't, and we'd still got the job done. New Zealand, the hosts, were to be our final opponents. While we had done what had been expected of us, a mounting injury list – which now included Helena – was a growing concern.

To be involved in a World Cup final at the age of 23 was something that excited me. Above all else, it was a huge honour. I knew from the start of the week that Helena's injury meant she wouldn't be involved. It was a cruel blow for her to miss out on the biggest game any player can ever play in. But I'd gone from not being sure of my position in the team to knowing I would be starting a World Cup final. You have to be prepared for injuries at major tournaments. World Cups are all about high pressure, and the bigger the games get, the more brutal they are.

Playing New Zealand in a World Cup final in front of a sold-out Eden Park was a new prospect for all the England players. The Black Ferns had gone through a remarkable turnaround ahead of their home World Cup, improving very quickly after making the canny decision to hire coaching guru Wayne Smith. Before Smith's arrival, they had been struggling for form and

CHAPTER 7

weren't getting the results they should have, given the quality of their team. They were packed with talent, so we were never going to be taking them lightly. But the fact the Canada semi-final had been so close meant there was definitely an edge to the camp environment in the week of the final.

In the build-up to the World Cup, the omission from the squad of scrum-half Mo Hunt had created lots of headlines, given her status as an experienced player. Midds had selected Leanne Infante and Lucy Packer as his two main scrum-halves, with Claudia Moloney-MacDonald covering No. 9 as well as wing. In the days leading up to the New Zealand game it became clear that both Leanne and Lucy were struggling for fitness. Leanne was named to start regardless, but Hannah Botterman and Helena Rowland had to miss out. On the morning of the final, Leanne had to withdraw. Her joints were too swollen to play. Lucy, who had been suffering with ankle ligament damage and wasn't initially named in the 23-player squad, now found herself starting. Claudia acted as scrum-half bench cover. We were being tested, and our preparation hadn't been perfect given the number of injuries, but we still believed we had the ability and strength in depth across the board – even without key players – to win.

The 2022 World Cup final should, in my opinion, be remembered as one of the greatest games of rugby the sport has ever seen. And that's men's and women's. It was that good. A crowd of 42,579 was the biggest in history for a women's international. We knew the atmosphere was going to be electric and that we were taking on the Black Ferns at what is seen as the

FINAL HEARTBREAK

home of New Zealand rugby. We'd prepared for the noise by making sure that our on-field communication was clear and concise. It needed to be because it was by far the largest crowd I'd played in front of and the incredible noise of the spectators meant it was hard to hear what the player next to you was saying. But I saw that as a reason to be positive, not negative. I scored inside three minutes.

We made a brilliant start and when Emily Scarratt passed me the ball, I didn't have to do much beyond apply the finish. A try in my first World Cup final was barely believable. Ten minutes later, Amy Cokayne was driven over for our second – we were 14-0 up and the Eden Park crowd had quietened down a little. It certainly helped settle a few of my nerves.

And then the game changed completely.

In the 18th minute, our wing Lydia Thompson was sent off for a dangerous tackle on superstar New Zealand back Portia Woodman-Wickliffe, who was forced off injured as a result of her blow to the head. In such a situation, you have to quickly accept that rugby can throw you a curveball. The game isn't always fair, and the key thing is not to moan about it but react and problem-solve as quickly as possible. We had a lot of that to do as the red card meant we had to play 62 minutes of the match with 14 players. We'd prepared as best we could for every possible match scenario that could have been thrown at us. That included injuries and a player being sent off.

Doing that in training is one thing. But reacting to losing a player in the pressure of a World Cup final is another entirely. You can do all the preparation in the world. But the truth is that,

CHAPTER 7

at 23, I didn't have as much experience as the players around me. Losing Lydia on the wing meant that my role as a full-back had to change, specifically in terms of covering space when we didn't have the ball. Being down to 14 players for so long meant I had to do a lot more running, and I didn't make the right calls at the right times. I remember a message coming on from the coaches via the physio after Lydia was sent off. We'd have more ground to cover defensively and as the full-back, my positioning had to change. I was told by the coaches that I was to stand in the front line of the defence when there was a scrum or line-out. But in open play, I was asked to drop back to cover the space if New Zealand kicked. It was a lot to take in, especially with a baying Kiwi crowd. It wasn't that I was underprepared, it was just that I wasn't as good as I could have been, at that age, at adapting to different circumstances as they played out in front of me. That only comes with experience and, in 2022, I didn't have lots of it.

With Lydia off the field, the Black Ferns started to get a lot of joy on the edges of the field because of their numerical advantage. It meant they soon came back into the game. Our problems continued to mount. Forward Zoe Stratford (née Aldcroft), who was a key figure, had to be taken off with a head injury. Considering everything that had gone against us up to that point, a 26-19 lead at half time was a good position. When you're playing in a World Cup final, your only focus is on doing the job as well as you can, to help your team win the trophy. You're not thinking about the spectators and what they're making of the game. But as the second half of the final swung back and forth, I don't think anyone watching, whether at Eden Park or on television, could have complained about the quality of the entertainment.

It was rugby of the highest order. Both teams swapped tries, Amy completing a hat-trick. Claudia came on for Lucy at scrum-half. Midds also substituted Sarah Hunter and Marlie Packer, which was significant as they were two of our most experienced players. Sarah was captain and Marlie was another key figure in the pack. Even a player down, we were never out of the game. New Zealand kept coming, though, and when the match clock ticked past 80 minutes and entered the red zone, we were three points behind.

Our backs were to the wall, but, crucially, we had field position. Our line-out and rolling maul had been our bread and butter for that whole World Cup. It was our go-to move. No one had been able to stop our forwards from the set-piece, not even New Zealand. Amy's treble in the final, along with a try from Marlie, had all come from the maul. So, when we had a line-out on the Black Ferns' five-metre line and Lark Atkin-Davies – on as a replacement for Amy – was getting ready to throw in, I thought to myself: 'S***. We've done it.' All tournament we'd scored from that position. I expected us to win the set-piece and drive over the line. I probably had space on the edge, but I didn't even call for it because I was waiting for the forwards to do what they do best. They'd done it all World Cup, so why should now be any different? I was stood out on the opposite side of the field when Lark threw the ball in. Abbie Ward was the target, but for pretty much the first time all tournament, and at the worst possi-

CHAPTER 7

ble moment, the throw didn't quite hit the mark. New Zealand's Joanah Ngan-Woo got up in the air to steal the ball from Abbie. As an edge player, I couldn't do anything to stop it. I couldn't run in and join the maul or try and reclaim possession. I was helpless. When referee Hollie Davidson blew the final whistle, I immediately felt numb.

We'd lost.

For the next five minutes or so, the reality of losing our 30-match unbeaten run in the game that mattered most simply wouldn't sink in. It was only when I saw how heartbroken the rest of the girls were that the numbness subsided and a feeling of desolation took over. I just thought to myself: 'No. It can't be over. We really need another shot at this. Can we not just go again?' We got back into the changing rooms.

Everyone was distraught. There was a common thought among all the players that it wasn't supposed to have ended like that. Alongside the feelings of sadness and disappointment was an element of guilt. So much had been expected of us at that World Cup, particularly from inside our own team. But tens of thousands of miles away, back at home, we knew there were people getting up early in the morning to watch our matches – all with the hope that we'd come back with the trophy. I felt like we'd let the next generation down, because I really believe that we could have changed women's rugby there and then if we had won that tournament.

The Lionesses had done just that with women's football, by winning the Euros, but we'd been unable to follow suit. It was devastating, but I don't believe Lydia's sending-off was the reason we didn't win the World Cup. Even with 14 players, we played well enough to win. As tough as it was to take, it was a loss that would ultimately make us stronger.

We'd lost a World Cup final, but there was no way we weren't going to go out partying that night. The match took place in the evening, so we didn't get back to the team hotel until late. We had a quick turnaround before heading out for drinks in Auckland. Some people might say we shouldn't have gone out because we didn't lift the trophy. I disagree with that. As much as we're all competitive professional athletes and winning is what counts, my view was that we'd still come second in a World Cup, and there was cause for celebration there. Of course, we were bitterly disappointed not to win. But we'd been in camp for so long together and worked so hard that we had to let off some steam. We made sure we had a good night, but I knew that early the next morning, and before our flight home, we had something else in the calendar.

A week or so before the final, I was one of several girls in the squad to book in for a bungee jump off Auckland Bridge. It was the biggest bungee jump in New Zealand. Obviously, there was no way we could do something like that while we still had matches to play, but once they were done we were given permission to go for it. The only problem was that in order to be able to do it before our flight home, we had to leave the hotel at six o'clock in the morning. When my alarm went off, I was still drunk from the night before and had only managed a few hours of sleep. It was probably a good job that I was still under the influence, because I had so much confidence doing the jump.

CHAPTER 7

It was still terrifying. We had to jump in weight order. Because I was the lightest of the girls in the group, I went last. It meant I could see everyone go ahead of me and they were all, understandably, very nervous at doing the jump. I was scared too. I'm an adrenaline seeker, something that started when I jumped off those cliffs in Portugal as a child. But the truth is, I'm terrified of heights. I'm terrified of lots of things, actually. I absolutely hate rollercoasters and insects.

Despite that, I was determined not to look scared. Not outwardly at least.

The man in charge at the top of the bridge told us that after we'd jumped off, it was unlikely we'd end up going into the water when we reached the bottom. But he also said it was more likely if you were relaxed as you went through the air. If you managed that, there was a small chance the water might graze your head. Trying to be a crowd pleaser, I jumped so confidently. I stuck out my arms like the Christ the Redeemer statue in Rio de Janeiro and fell forwards. On the surface it looked like I was loving every minute. But the reality was different. It was so, so scary. I tumbled through the air, travelling not only all the way down to the sea water below, but being totally submerged by it. At one point, as I was underwater, I genuinely thought the bungee rope had snapped. It certainly felt like I was drowning.

It was probably only a matter of seconds, but it felt like I was underwater for ages. Thankfully, I came back up and lived to tell the tale. It was an interesting way for my World Cup to end. I don't think I'd do a bungee again, definitely not after a big night out.

But that jump was certainly good for one thing.

The adrenaline rush of the fall and cold-water plunge sobered me up straight away and meant I was able to fly home without the added pain of a hangover.

8

England's New Dawn

There's a running joke between me and those who know me best about how obsessed I am with my notepads. I'll happily admit that obsessed is exactly what I am. I love to write things down, which is all a big change from my first England camp when I didn't even know I needed to take a notepad to meetings. Most people write notes in order not to forget things. But I'm different. I read once that some people write things down in order to forget them, and that really resonated with me. That's exactly what I need to do. I feel emotions deeply. I'm very empathetic. I don't know how many other people reading this will feel the same as me, but the main reason I write things down is to clear my brain and to get certain things out of my head so I can move on. That might seem bonkers, but it's just how my brain works.

The reason I bring this up is because after we lost the 2022 World Cup final to New Zealand, my mind was just filled with thoughts and feelings. For me, the journey to the 2025 World Cup started as soon as the whistle went that night at Eden Park. It was a heartbreaking moment. We had a 36-hour flight home from New Zealand. That's a lot of time to think and write notes,

CHAPTER 8

so I got to work. I was determined to find ways to improve, so I would never again feel the pain of losing a game like that. Not when it mattered most.

I wanted to get down on paper all the little things that I might be able to improve in both my life and on-field performance. The first thing I thought of was sleep. Was I getting enough of it? If not, how could I get better sleep? Maybe by using a better mattress? If so, what brand could I partner with to get one? On the field, could my kicking game improve? I wanted to be able to kick more consistently, so did I need to connect with a new kicking coach? I knew I was already very fast and had a strong running and attacking game. But how could I get even faster? I drew a massive spider diagram, detailing all the little 1 per cent improvements that I thought would put me in a better place for the 2025 World Cup. The exercise was almost like drawing a line under the 2022 tournament, getting it out of my head, and moving on with a new plan to live by.

Sat in the economy seats on the plane home, I was thinking to myself: 'We've got three years now until the next World Cup. What's going to happen in that time and what can I do to make sure I don't have the same gut-wrenching feeling I do currently?' It was about creating a new start point to move forward from. I asked myself if I could have done more or if I had been in the best position I could have been for the New Zealand World Cup. On the whole, I concluded the answer was yes. We couldn't have done anything else. I really, truly believe that.

But, at the same time, I knew I could get better. I still believe that now. I'm always open to opportunities that can make me both a better player and a better person. Note taking, I find, is really helpful. I'd recommend it to anyone. It helps me appreciate the place that I'm in right now, but also what's to come in the future. On the way back from New Zealand, it was difficult to look too far ahead. Our mood was so bleak, we might as well have been in a morgue, especially on the first leg from Auckland to Dubai. It was only as we transferred in the Middle East that the girls finally started to talk to each other.

A few days after I got home, and once the jetlag had worn off, I looked at the notes I'd made on the flight. I acted on a lot of them. But there were also many others I didn't. I don't see that as a negative, though. I look at that positively and see it as exciting. There are still things I can improve on? Great, how good is that?

One of things I did do was to start working consistently with Andy Holloway, a kicking coach. Andy has also worked with us at the Red Roses and had previously been with Ealing. He's outstanding and has made a real difference to my game. I also took my gym work a lot more seriously, in a bid to improve strength and power in my lower body. I worked a lot on my split squat and RDL exercises. These are lower leg exercises that focus on improving strength and power. I noticed quite quickly they made a big difference to my game. I put on some weight, which was a big benefit, and I started seeing a good relationship with food as essential to my career, which was something I didn't do previously. My diet became a lot better and I moved past the problems I'd encountered with food during the time of the Covid-19 pandemic. I ate better and more consistently,

CHAPTER 8

and it was at this time that I started to have plain pasta as my pre-match meal. I also worked closely with the England team to increase my nutrient intake, using things like protein shots. They were little fixes, but the impact of them was significant. I did specific sprint work for a few weeks, focusing on my technique and posture. The aim was to maximise the efficiency of my running technique and I really enjoyed it. The problem was I couldn't find the time in my calendar to do it consistently, because those sessions were based in Loughborough and the travel there and back made regular visits difficult. Although the sprint work fell by the wayside, I knew that better nutrition and the strength I was gaining from my gym work would mean I'd get even faster. That's exactly what happened.

By the start of 2024, a year out from the next World Cup, my game was in a very good place. There was also a fresh start for England. John Mitchell had taken over as head coach from Simon Middleton. After the disappointment of the 2022 World Cup, Midds had stayed in charge for the 2023 Six Nations. The Grand Slam-sealing win over France was his last game as coach.

Midds has been a massive part of my career. He challenged me in ways that definitely made me the player I am today. We go back a long, long way. Midds gave me my England debut as a teenager in 2017, but our journey actually started way before that. I was only at Castleford for a couple of months while I was playing youth rugby and played just a handful of games with Midds' daughter Cara, but we did overlap, and Midds would come to some of those matches. We obviously had a great relationship, but I've never felt as if I owe him, or indeed anybody, anything. I don't like to think about, or see, life like that. For me, you're never in debt to somebody. If they give you an opportunity – as Midds did with me – it's because they trust your ability to take their career and the team's journey in a positive direction. It's a transaction. That's it. I've always wanted to become the best player I can be. And if you always have that attitude, I think you will perform to your best.

I try not to get involved with politics in professional sport. I understand that coaches come and go in the same way that players come and go. All you can focus on is delivering your best. You can't control what happens further up the food chain, with coaches or in the boardroom. I could have said I didn't want Midds to leave. But he did. I couldn't control it. I could say the same about Mitch and maybe one day he will leave too. You've just got to be okay with change. And I think at that time, with or without Midds, we were a team that was on its way to fantastic things, even with the New Zealand loss factored in. Midds had been there for a long time – since 2015. He'd accomplished so much. But Mitch gave us a freshness and a new start. It was a case of the baton being passed on. Mitch handled that handover brilliantly. When he came in for the first time, he basically said: 'I've got some huge boots to fill. But I'm just going to wear some new trainers.' I thought that was a great way of putting it. He was not trying to replace Midds directly. He was going to do things his own way. He didn't work like Midds. The two both do very good things in their own right. But they're very, very different characters and have very, very different methods.

CHAPTER 8

Everyone knew about Mitch. He'd done it all in the men's game, coaching the All Blacks and working with England as an assistant to Eddie Jones, among a number of other roles. His last job before joining us was as an assistant with Japan at the 2023 men's World Cup. There was no doubting his coaching calibre. But he was coming into the women's game for the first time, and that left us not quite knowing what to expect.

We needn't have worried. After Mitch was finished with Japan, he joined us for the WXV tournament at the end of 2023, a newly created competition that was a bit like the World Cup, only with the teams divided into different tiers based on their quality. Louis Deacon – or 'Deacs' – is the man in charge of our forwards, but he had become our interim coach when Midds left. Mitch joined us for the latter stages of WXV and, although he wasn't technically coaching, he was around the group. I distinctly remember the first conversation I had with him in New Zealand. We went on to win the WXV tournament by beating the Black Ferns 33-12 in Auckland. It was revenge of sorts for our World Cup final defeat a year earlier in the same city. But I wasn't thinking about that. For me and the team, the focus was on the present and an exciting future under Mitch. At half time in the final, Mitch came into the changing room. I said to him: 'Are you seeing anything?' I wanted to gauge his opinion on the game, my performance and how we could improve for the second 40. 'What's your instinct?' he responded. I said: 'What do you mean?' Mitch then said: 'Well, whatever you're seeing on the pitch, I back that and I trust that. You just need to go out there and trust yourself and go for it 100 per cent because, at the moment, you're going at about 70 per cent.' A conversation that lasted just a matter of seconds immediately unlocked a completely new part of my game. It was a crucial moment.

Having coaches like Mitch and Lou Meadows come into the system and say 'just be you' has honestly been the biggest blessing I've had as a rugby player. Lou was our attack coach, having taken over from Scott Bemand. The messages delivered by Mitch and Lou have allowed me to learn, go from strength to strength and play not only a brand of rugby that suits me, but one I can keep on getting better at.

From that point on, I decided to totally back myself on the field and play on instinct. My new mantra was not to overthink things, and to go for broke. It was a huge turning point for me and gave me real confidence that my game could go to another level. Growing up, I was always told: 'We want you to be like that person or that person.' But when Mitch came in, he said: 'I want you to just be you.' My rugby since then has skyrocketed.

I've had a great relationship with all my coaches, if I'm honest. But the ones I really get on with best are the ones that take on a father- or mother-type role. It doesn't matter to me if they're a man or a woman. You know the way your parents are with you? It's like that. My parents are honest with me. I know they have my best intentions at heart, but we have frank and challenging conversations. They're prepared to tell me the sun's not shining all the time. Equally, they hand down praise when it's deserved.

I think that's the way it should be and that's kind of the relationship I have with Mitch. I had that with Midds too. In fact, all the coaches that have really helped my development in becoming the player and person that I am today have tended to act in almost a parental way. I'm not quite sure why that is. I guess part of it is down to the fact I started playing for England at such a young age. Other players might not like to be treated in the same way. It's different for everyone and that's what makes a team environment so good. I think it also makes a coach's job really difficult. As a coach, you have to adapt how you do your job depending on the individuals you're working with.

As a key assistant under Mitch, Deacs provided continuity from the Midds era. And, after retiring as a player, Sarah Hunter also joined Mitch's coaching staff. Sarah is a Red Roses legend. She was a phenomenal captain and a huge inspiration to us all in the squad, especially the younger players. She helped lay the platform for what the women's game in England is today. She'd won everything and knew what it took to lift a World Cup. I definitely looked up to her, and her transition into coaching was seamless.

When Mitch came in, he spoke in the media about making the Red Roses into a more expansive team. At the 2022 World Cup, and at the end of Midds's time in charge, one criticism we faced – despite our success – was that our game plan was too forward-dominated. The argument was that we had a good rolling maul, but not much else. I didn't buy that, partly because I always try to ignore all the outside noise. Whatever your coach's plans are, and whether you agree with them or not, at the end of the day, that's your coach and you have to trust in what they're doing. They're in charge.

ENGLAND'S NEW DAWN

With Mitch, I could definitely sense he wanted to make us a more well-rounded team. Mitch is a very knowledgeable and experienced coach, and he obviously knew what we were good at. Even though we didn't win the 2022 World Cup, we'd shown in New Zealand we had a very strong forward pack. There was no doubt the driving maul was one of our biggest weapons. But Mitch also placed emphasis on other parts of our game he thought we could excel at. We have a back-line in which almost everyone can kick. We've got players that are elusive and fast, but also players that are strong and powerful. What was great about Mitch was that he built a team and wider squad where he encouraged everyone to identify and deliver on their super strengths. Things progressed very quickly.

We'd ended 2023 – which had been a transitional coaching year – with a perfect record and, on the back of WXV, we went into the 2024 Six Nations excited to begin a new era. It was a fantastic Championship.

It wasn't the first Six Nations or Grand Slam we'd won. But we did it playing a brand of rugby that was so enjoyable to be a part of. It was one of those campaigns where we just knew we were going to be successful. You could sense it from the very start. I never had any doubt we'd achieve a clean sweep, even with a new coaching set-up, because our training and the atmosphere in camp was so good. I just really, really enjoyed the first six months of 2024. In fact, the whole year was pretty amazing. It didn't feel like we had pressure on us and that mantra to play with freedom came from Mitch. We were putting the ball through the backs but also smashing it up

CHAPTER 8

with the forwards. And it felt like everyone enjoyed being in the team environment. At the same time, all of the players knew we still had a lot more to give. It was hugely exciting knowing we could perform the way we were, while also being aware we had room to get even better.

When I look back on that campaign now, it makes me so happy. It was the first time that we were genuinely smiling on the pitch. I loved that tournament. The back three I've played with most with the England team has seen Jess Breach and Abby Dow as the two wings, alongside me as the full-back. As a trio, our collective strength was running and attacking, and in the 2024 Six Nations the forwards provided us with an incredible platform. We were only finishing off what they started. The tries and wins started to mount up. For the first time, we really felt like we were on a roll. When that happens, it's a weird sensation, because you kind of just go with it. When you're in a good moment, you don't overthink things. If you're playing games and big competitions, sometimes you don't really notice exactly what's going on until you step outside of the team environment. That's how intense England camps are. You're just so focused.

At that time, we probably matured into knowing what our strong points were, and we had several strings to our bow. We'd very quickly become a multi-dimensional team. I remember saying in interviews during that Six Nations: 'Good luck to any team facing us, because if you think you can get us in the forwards, we'll get you in the backs. If you think you can get us in the backs, we'll surprise you and use our power game or kicking game.'

We became a squad that was able to find a way to beat any opponent we came up against. The strength we had was not just from 1 to 15. It was from 1 to 23, and even beyond that. The depth in the squad was something to be reckoned with. It was a really cool place to be in, knowing that anyone could step into the shirt and do the job in their own way. I think that was the key thing. No one was trying to play like anybody else, but we all performed our roles within a clear team structure and game plan.

Personally, I felt in fantastic form. In that campaign, I told myself that every time I found a gap, I should just go for it. And I did. On the back of that conversation with Mitch in New Zealand, that was my new approach, and it paid off big time. I had to get my fitness and speed up to play that style of game, but the extra gym work I'd done the previous year certainly helped on that front. We beat Italy 48-0, Wales 46-10 and Scotland 46-0. Then we returned to Allianz Stadium and beat Ireland 88-10 in front of a crowd of 48,778. It was a sign of what was to come in terms of the huge growth in attendances for our matches. I ended with a hat-trick, scoring three of our 14 tries. That game set up a Grand Slam decider with France in Bordeaux on the Championship's final weekend.

Beating France away is always a huge moment. It's obviously a privilege to play any Grand Slam game. But to do so in France is extra special. They're our biggest rivals in the Six Nations because of the levels of performance they can reach. On home soil, the French fans create an incredible atmosphere, as I first found out in Grenoble in 2018. The rivalry between

CHAPTER 8

the two teams, in both in the men's and women's games, has historically been so intense. But in that match, our mantra of playing without pressure paid off. We'd played in Grand Slam matches before so knew what to expect. Obviously, having those past experiences does help. But we knew that every time you play a game of rugby, it's going to be a different story. And for that France match, we just had to write a new story. While still being very much where our feet were, we knew that, with a home World Cup around the corner, the 42-21 win was part of a bigger picture. There was still so much more to come from us as a team but also, for me as an individual, there was an entirely new challenge.

9
Becoming an Olympian

It never happened for me in 2021. But driven on by missing out on the Tokyo Games, the burning desire to become an Olympian never left me. So, once Mitch had taken over from Midds as England head coach, I thought I would see if I could try my luck for the Paris Olympics of 2024. I didn't know Mitch before he came in, but my understanding of him from quite early on was that he wants the best for his players. And I also thought to myself: 'You know what? He doesn't know that I signed to play for the 15s only, so I might as well just ask him if there's a chance.' That's exactly what I did.

Towards the end of the Six Nations of 2024, I sat down with Mitch. I was open, honest and I told him I was interested in going back to sevens for the next Olympics. We had an off-season at the time of the Games, so I thought it was doable. It wasn't like I had to choose between one or the other, as I had done in the past. I was also fortunate to have had a good Six Nations, which I thought might help my cause!

Mitch's message was very clear. He said: 'Well, I'll give you a few days. I want you to put a case together as to why you think you should be able to transfer over to the sevens. What benefits

CHAPTER 9

can it give you? But also, what are the cons? What could possibly go wrong and what are the things we'll need to manage? Come to me with those things and I'll let you know.'

So, I went away and made a bit of a list, as I often tend to do. On the whole, I only saw benefits from playing in the Olympics and I pointed out the following to Mitch:

1. With the sevens, I'd get to train at a very, very high standard in a different set-up with people that were also just as fast and dynamic as I am.
2. I'd get to train throughout the off-season, so I'd stay fit.
3. Should I make the team, I'd be playing in front of huge crowds, which would mean I'd be used to those environments and high-pressure games for the 2025 15s World Cup.
4. I wanted to do Great Britain proud.
5. As ever, I'd try my hardest to do something really great on the field and bid for an Olympic medal.

After some discussion, Mitch gave me the green light to try out with the Great Britain team. That didn't mean Olympic selection was guaranteed. Far from it, in fact. But I was very grateful to be given the chance.

At the end of the 2024 Six Nations Grand Slam, I joined back up with the sevens programme. It was very hard work. I've always loved the shorter format of rugby. With only 14 players on the pitch at any one time instead of 30 in the full, 15-a-side game, there is clearly a lot more space. That suits my game, with its pace and footwork. But sevens is also an incredibly difficult sport. With so much more ground to cover, the fitness side is incredibly hard. In sevens, your repeat sprints must be really, really strong, and you're constantly moving. In 15s rugby, there are moments when you can have a break. But not in sevens. And, fitness aside, what I also found difficult was assimilating into a team that was already quite established. By that, I don't mean the culture of the side or anything around the squad environment, because all the girls and everyone in the coaching set-up were lovely to me. I was made to feel so welcome. But, as I've already mentioned, in the wake of the pandemic financial pressures dictated that instead of individual unions the sevens had become a combined Great Britain team. It meant that while I knew some of the players in the team from my past sevens experience with England, I also had to get to know others for the first time, and very quickly too. This was crucial to us being successful as a team.

As well as making personal connections with my new teammates, I also had to understand them as players. Minute things were vital. I had to get to know, for example, how far Isla Norman-Bell could pass off both her left and right hands. How quick is Grace Crompton? How much space do I need to give her? How far does Emma Uren travel laterally before getting a defender to bite? These were all small things we had to focus on during training. Still, we had a really talented squad – one that also included my England 15s teammate Megan Jones and the Wales wing Jasmine Joyce-Butchers. In the build-up to Paris, I played sevens in Madrid, as well as a tournament in Hamburg.

CHAPTER 9

Doing so was an essential part of my Olympic preparation and allowed me to get a better feel for my teammates and the squad environment. The Germany trip was extra special because my brother Sam was playing for Great Britain's men's side at the same event. With my parents coming out to watch both their children represent Great Britain with the family name of Kildunne on the backs of their shirts, it was a very proud moment for us all.

If I were to play at another Olympics – and that is something I would like to do in Los Angeles in 2028 – then in an ideal world, I would like to play more than two warm-up tournaments to get a better grasp of everything around me. But that was the situation pre-Paris – we had no choice other than to get on with it.

To make the final squad for the Olympics was a dream. It was officially announced on 19 June, but we knew we'd be told before that whether we were in or out. I was at home in my kitchen in Reading when I first received a text message from our coach Ciaran Beattie. It confirmed my Olympic dream was going to become a reality. I just couldn't believe it. I'd had a race against time to prove my worth, but had managed to do so. Because I knew when we were due to receive the selection news, I filmed my own reaction in real time. The clip is still on my Instagram. It's worth a watch if you haven't seen it because I cried my eyes out. The waterworks started because, even though I'd had a good year, Olympic selection was far from guaranteed. It doesn't matter how good you are in 15s, or how successful you've been in a season, stepping into a new team that's been training really hard for the past few years – and they were a brilliant team – was always going to be tough. But I'd made it and I was going to live out another of my lifelong dreams. I just kept saying to myself over and over in my head: 'S***! I'm going to become an Olympian.' After the initial text, we each got a call from Ciaran, which was a nice personal touch.

We travelled out to Paris on the Eurostar. When we walked through St Pancras to get to the train, we were all wearing our Team GB kit. There were thousands of people there to see us off, all applauding and waving Great Britain flags. It showed me how big it was to be going to an Olympics.

The sevens was one of the first events at the Games. To start with, we were based for a week in a holding camp just outside Paris. It was a base for all Team GB athletes, regardless of the sport you played. As one group departed to head to the Olympic Village proper, another would arrive. As the rugby teams left – both men's and women's – the athletics group was coming in. It felt like you were part of something incredibly special – one overall team united by the same desire to come back with as many medals as possible.

While we were in the holding camp, we didn't really know what to expect from the Olympic Village. When we moved in, a week before the rugby started, I couldn't believe my eyes. It was one of the coolest things I've ever seen. You know the computer game *The Sims* – the one where you build houses, villages, towns and cities? That's how I'd best describe the Olympic Village. It was like living in some sort of simulation. It honestly didn't feel like real life. It felt otherworldly somehow, cut off from the rest

CHAPTER 9

of the planet, a place where everyone you locked eyes with was an elite athlete. It was a little bit weird, to be honest.

Each nation had their separate block – Team GB, Australia, Fiji and the rest. They all had their respective flags outside, so you'd know who was in which block. Everyone was always in their team kit and almost everyone cycled everywhere. You'd be able to identify an athlete's country because of the clothing they wore, and yet you had no idea what sport they played. I'd never speak to other groups, but when I walked past one, I'd size them up. I loved the game of looking at the athletes and trying to guess what their sport was. What did they play? Was it fencing? Or were they swimmers or boxers? It intrigued me no end.

I also loved the pin swapping, which played right into my creative and fashion side. Collecting pins is an Olympic tradition that dates back to 1896 and is a way of getting souvenirs to remember your participation in the Games. You'd stick them on your rucksack or your clothes. As Great Britain athletes, we were given pins of our own, some of which we'd exchange with athletes from other countries. The Olympic Village was like a playground for big children. I was a regular visitor to the ice cream van. You could go up and take whatever you wanted. It was the same with a Costa van, where you could get coffee. You didn't have to pay for anything.

Then there were the canteens. The size of them was just crazy and they quickly blew up on social media. The main canteen was huge and had over 3,000 seats. I didn't like going to that one, if I'm honest. It was too big for me, plus the smaller canteen was closer to our block.

I shared a room with Abi Burton, who was one of the two reserves who had travelled with our 12-player squad. When we entered our rooms in the village for the first time, there were presents waiting for us as Olympic athletes. Again, all free. There was a lottery ticket. I opened that straight away, but sadly didn't win. We all received special Olympic mobile phones, too. They were flip phones, a proper throwback, which I was a big fan of as I like my retro style. We also got a special Olympic coin and printed towels. There was just so much stuff. There were free beauty areas where you could get your hair and nails done, as well as a games room with things like snooker and darts and photo booths. When it got dark, the whole place was lit up by LED lighting.

We had so much kit. Before we went to Paris we all had to attend a big kitting-out day with Adidas. We went from room to room, trying countless different items on. It wasn't just playing and training kit, it was also the outfits you'd wear in your spare time and around the village. You never really wore your own clothes. With Team GB, we'd have what were called 'green days', 'blue days' and 'red days'. The women's sevens players were on a huge group chat with all the different athletes. Each morning, there would be a message on the group to say what colour day it was. But what was really cool was that there were loads of different clothing choices, so everyone could create their own style. For example, if the text said it was a 'red day', you had to wear red but could choose which items you wore – for example a t-shirt or polo. I really liked the creative aspect of it.

One of the best bits of the Olympics was sharing facilities with athletes you would never normally come across. As

CHAPTER 9

a rugby player, you only ever really see people like you on a day-to-day basis. You might every so often mingle with athletes from other sports, but only at events or commercial appearances. In Paris, the rugby players all mixed in with everyone else and that included some high-profile celebrities. Tom Daley, the top diver who retired after the Games, was someone I walked past quite a few times. I had to pinch myself a little bit. I was too scared to say hello. The same thing happened with Sir Andy Murray. I mean no offence to Murray when I say this, because he's a proper tennis legend, but when he turned up at the village for the first time, he had quite long hair and a bit of a beard. By the time the opening ceremony came around, I didn't even recognise him. He'd shaved, cut his hair and was like a different man!

One day he was just casually sat next to me having a cup of tea. I was never going to ask him for a picture or anything like that. But I texted my mum to say: 'Andy Murray is sat next to me!' At the time, you take things like that in your stride. But when I look back on it now, it feels like it was someone else sat there and I'm telling you about a friend of mine that was in the Olympic Village, not my own experiences. I still have to constantly remind myself that person was in fact me.

Ahead of the sevens tournament beginning, we had a special shirt presentation. It's something we do before every England match in 15s and involves the players being given the jersey they'll wear in the match. But with it being the Olympics, this one felt different. Ahead of the Games, there were lots of strikes on the Eurostar, which caused severe travel disruption to fans who wanted to get to Paris. They certainly impacted my mum and dad's travel, to such an extent that they told me they thought they wouldn't be able to make it to the shirt presentation. I knew they'd arrive in time for the matches, but I didn't expect them to be at the event, which all the players' families had been invited to. When I got to the room for what was supposed to be a really proud moment, I was actually feeling a little bit sad. I wanted my family to be there. One by one the other players all started to get up to receive their shirts, which were presented to them by one of their loved ones, who said a few words. I didn't know who was going to present mine because, after all, my family were caught up in the travel chaos. What I didn't know was that my mum had been hiding in a corner the whole time. She had made it after all. When she jumped out to present me with my shirt, the shock and emotion of seeing her made me cry my eyes out like a little baby. She'd got lucky with the trains. My dad and brother had to get a ferry over instead, but they got there eventually. My mum wasn't really ready to give a speech. I think she was just so tired from trying to get over to Paris in time. But she said how proud she was of me, and that I was just a young girl from Yorkshire who was living out her dreams. She said she couldn't believe the journey that I'd been on. It was a very special moment for us both, the only shame being that my dad and brother couldn't be there. At the presentation, I also played a video I'd put together of our team's journey to the Olympics. I hadn't been with the side that long, but when I first joined, three months before the Games, I started capturing video content. I edited it all together to show everyone how far we'd

CHAPTER 9

come. It was a lovely way for us to prepare for the moment we'd all been waiting for.

Because the women's rugby sevens started the day after the opening ceremony, we didn't attend the traditional start to the Games. Our focus had to be on performance, so we couldn't be on our feet for long periods. But before all the athletes departed for the ceremony, I made sure to walk around the village. I took pictures of them all in their different outfits. It absolutely hammered it down, so much it broke my camera. But it was amazing to see all the different countries and cultures of the world collide in a sporting environment. The men's rugby sevens had taken place before the Olympics had even begun. The big story was Antoine Dupont – who is one of if not the best male player in the world – moving from 15s to sevens to help his country France win gold at a home Games. To witness that, and the scale of the interest in rugby's shorter format, showed how big sevens can be. As a player who, like Dupont, had moved from 15s to sevens for the Olympics, I was determined to also make a big impression. But when the action began, I don't think the results we achieved reflected how good we were as a team. Sevens is such a tough game.

The narrative female rugby has had to contend with for almost the entirety of my career is that the women's game is always lagging behind the men's. It's pretty much all I've known. A narrative is just an expectation based on history, so I do understand it to a degree. It's the same with the Red Roses. There's a narrative that we're always expected to win. But that's only based on what we've done in the last three years. The narrative we'd heard ahead of the women's sevens in Paris was that while the men's games would be sold out – and they were – there wouldn't be as many people there for our matches. The Stade de France was full to the brim for the men's matches, culminating with France and Dupont taking home gold medals. When the women's tournament started, we didn't know what to expect.

But we needn't have worried. One of the most important things that drives me in my career is being an individual who breaks new boundaries, and in doing so helps to do the same for the women's game as a whole. That's what happened in Paris. We warmed up for matches behind the scenes at the Stade de France, in an area from where you couldn't see the pitch or the stands. It was a bit like having a backstage pass to *Britain's Got Talent* – something I'd dreamed of as a kid when I used to watch the show. As we were getting ready to line up and run out before our first game against Ireland, we couldn't initially see how many people were inside the venue. Then we came round the corner to see every seat full. It took my breath away. Truly, it did. My brain went into overdrive. My thoughts were: 'Wow, what is this? This isn't the narrative and this isn't what we know!' By the time we had got to the centre of the pitch and had come together for a team huddle, we all looked at each other and had a little giggle. Part of that was nervous energy. After all, we were about to play rugby in the Olympics. But I think a bigger part of it was that we'd had no idea what to expect in terms of crowd size. The huge number of fans who attended showed that the women's rugby can be as big as the men's. It certainly was at the 2024 Paris Olympics.

CHAPTER 9

Losing to the USA in the quarter-finals was a disappointment and meant we missed out on a medal, which was tough to take. Clearly, winning gold had been our target and it was something I felt we were capable of; I'm still motivated by the prospect of getting on the podium at some point in the future. But Paris 2024 will always remain a phenomenal sporting and personal experience for me, even if I felt I could have had more time on the field and given more as a result. I'm also well aware of how difficult sevens is. I've played the game a lot. You must be prepared for anything to happen.

An Olympics is the pinnacle of sporting competition and we were in a tough group alongside Australia, Ireland and South Africa. The other thing to remember is that a game of sevens is just 14 minutes long; it can be over very, very quickly. If your opponents score in the first few minutes of a 15-a-side game, you still have more than 70 minutes left to get back into the game. If that happens in sevens, it's only natural to think: 'S***, we've now only got 12 minutes to score.' If the opposition then scores again, that already short time only diminishes further and panic sets in even more. That's the thing with sevens. You can be the best team in the world, but if it's just not your day, there's no time to bring it back.

The team's performances were criticised on social media. That was hard to take, because we gave it our all. But I'm also aware that I probably never quite performed to my best on the field in Paris. I don't think I really had enough time to be fully prepared, having joined the team so soon after the Six Nations. There were just a couple of months between that and the

Olympics. But, having said that, I can't make excuses. I gave everything I could to win a medal. On that occasion, it just wasn't to be.

I've said it plenty of times before, but I always want to push myself to be a better player. I knew that doing the sevens was going to be tough. I also knew I wasn't going to walk into the team. But I did know it was going to make me fitter and give me experiences I couldn't get elsewhere. I believe you become a better player from gaining experience, but I've also said from day one that I don't want to acquire that experience by simply growing older. I've always wanted to capture opportunities when they're presented to me, run with them, and see where they take me. The Paris Olympics was a great example of exactly that. It wasn't just a stepping stone for me or a way of building for the World Cup. It was a separate thing in itself. I wanted to go to the Olympics. I still want to go to another Olympics. And that's not to make me the best 15s player, it's to say that I've won gold at an Olympics. I don't think that desire will leave me until I've achieved it.

Hopefully, one day that will happen. A career in professional sport is short, so I would hate to reach the end of mine thinking I'd missed an opportunity. I'm always going to be the sort of player who works hard to realise their ambitions. If that involves asking a tough question or pushing boundaries, then that's what I'll do.

As I was packing up and getting ready to leave Paris, the women's footballers were arriving in the Olympic Village. One of the first friends I made outside of school wasn't a rugby

CHAPTER 9

player. It was a girl called Grace Neville, who I met on holiday in Portugal when we used to go there all the time. I remember being in the pool, looking across, and seeing this girl doing constant kick-ups with a football. At that time, I thought I was playing a good level of football. I could do a few kick-ups. But Grace, even though she was still a teenager like me, was doing a LOT of kick-ups. I hadn't ever seen a girl keep a football in the air that long.

Grace and I ended up becoming really close that holiday, and we'd meet up when our families returned to Portugal. We're not as close now as we were in the past, but she texted me before the Olympics to say she was representing New Zealand in the women's football. It was not only nice to reconnect with her and relive the journeys that took us from two 14-year-old girls playing football on a Portuguese beach to both becoming Olympians, but also a great way for my Games to end. We'd both come a long way and that was something worth celebrating.

After my Olympics stint, I returned to 15s, where I ended 2024 with 14 tries in nine Tests for England. Nine of those scores came in the Six Nations and my performances – combined with the team winning the Grand Slam – meant I was named player of the tournament. It was a huge honour. For me, the team always comes first, but individual awards are great. On the back of that year's Six Nations, I was nominated for World Rugby's women's player of the year award. It was incredibly humbling. In fact, when the shortlist came out, it was a bit of an odd feeling. I got a call from Charlie Hayter, the head of women's performance at the RFU, to tell me I'd been nominated. It was a big moment for me. I knew I'd had a good season. But at the same time, my initial reaction to the news was that I didn't think I could be named world player of the year, as I still didn't feel as if I'd reached the limits of my potential.

I also knew that on the same weekend the awards were due to be held in Monaco, I had a huge game for Harlequins against our London rivals Saracens. The life of a professional athlete is full of decisions about which sacrifices you are prepared to make. You get offered lots and lots of really cool opportunities. But you can't do each and every one. At certain points, you have to wrestle with what sits well with you and what doesn't. The opportunity to go to Monaco for the World Rugby awards was clearly amazing. For many players it is a once-in-a-lifetime chance. But when Charlie told me I'd be on the guestlist as an award nominee, my first reaction was that, as great as that was, the Saracens game was more important. I was well aware of how big the match was, given our rivalry with Saracens. I wanted to help the team. So, when I was told I couldn't go to Monaco because the Saracens game had to be my first priority, I was okay with that. But then we had another conversation about it. Harlequins understood that the nomination was hugely prestigious and that this might be the only time in my career I was on the shortlist. They said they would be open to me going to Monaco and missing the Saracens match.

But this didn't sit well with me. I thought about how guilty I'd feel if, having travelled to Monaco, I didn't win the award and then Harlequins lost. So I told England and World Rugby that I wasn't going to go to Monaco. I'd made peace with that decision

CHAPTER 9

and was happy with it. After I'd informed the relevant people of my plans to play against Saracens instead, I tried to focus on the match. But, almost instantly, Charlie called back. I was stood in my living room at home when he broke the news to me that I *had* to go to Monaco because I'd won. I wasn't supposed to know this in advance and was sworn to secrecy – I was only allowed to tell my mum and dad – but they'd said to make sure I was definitely there in person. That moment was very, very special.

After I hung up, I had to take the time to process exactly what had just happened. It definitely took a while to sink in. In rugby, you live life in the fast lane and a lot of things pass you by. But this was a moment to sit still and take stock of what I'd achieved. I ended up going to Monaco, of course. I didn't have a choice. It was a crazy experience, one that didn't play out anywhere near like I'd planned.

I told the Harlequins girls I wasn't going to be playing against Saracens because I would be going to Monaco, but I couldn't tell them that I'd won. Only my club coaches had been told the truth by Charlie. I was worried about what my teammates were thinking deep down. I didn't want anyone to doubt my commitment to the team. We were booked to fly to France from Heathrow. But the weather really wasn't good and, on the day before we were scheduled to leave, the flight was cancelled due to high winds. All I could think to myself was 'S***. Now I'm not only going to miss the Saracens match, but also the awards because of the bloody wind!'

I'm not the sort of person to panic when things like that happen, but I think the people at World Rugby had a bit of a sweat on. The night before the awards, I was on Skyscanner searching for flights. It was proving difficult. My brain had only one thought: 'How the hell do I get out to Monaco now?' Then, in the early hours of the morning, I had a call from World Rugby to say they'd sorted something. I ended up getting a charter flight from Heathrow with a number of the men's South African players. Pieter-Steph du Toit (who ended up winning the men's award), Eben Etzebeth, Cheslin Kolbe and Ox Nché were all there. There were quite a few England women's players. Maddie Feaunati was there. So too was Holly Aitchison. All of us couldn't believe what was going on. It was just all so crazy. Being on a private jet made me feel like royalty. It was very surreal to have that sort of experience and a long way from growing up in West Yorkshire, that's for sure. I thought the private jet experience was going to be like some sort of James Bond-type experience. But it was literally just a smaller version of a normal plane, albeit one loaded with gigantic rugby players.

The best bit about it all, and something I would pay for in the future, was the private airport security you get with a charter flight. You fly from a separate part of the main airport at Heathrow, and when you wheel your bag in, someone takes it from you. Then you sit down. You can have food, a drink, or watch TV. You can basically do whatever you want and then about 20 minutes before the flight goes, they call you straight through security and on to the plane. Not a queue in sight.

When we got to Monaco, things happened very quickly. I managed to get two tickets originally, but I had three people coming out with me – my mum and dad, and my then boyfriend.

CHAPTER 9

My dad and boyfriend were just going to sit at the hotel while the ceremony was happening and then meet us afterwards for the party. But I was fortunate to be given two extra tickets, which was great as it meant all the people I was closest to were there. It was just the most amazing event, held at the Salle des étoiles, which is a concert hall in Monte Carlo. Frank Sinatra, Whitney Houston, Stevie Wonder, Shirley Bassey, Tina Turner and Elton John have all performed there in the past. There were thousands of people there. The champagne was flowing. My overriding memory is of people dressed as flamingos doing some dancing when we arrived. I'd never been to anything quite like it. My mum and dad definitely hadn't. For them to see me collect the award and give a speech surrounded by all the best rugby players on the planet was very surreal for us all. What was even better was that on the way to the awards I could watch the stream of the Harlequins–Saracens game on my phone. Harlequins beat Saracens in the dying minutes of the game! I always say that everything in life is written for us, and that day really showed that to be the case. Everything aligned just perfectly.

I don't really remember what I said when I collected the award. It's all a bit of a blur of flashing lights and popping cameras. But after I won, and in the few days that followed, I reconnected with a lot of my old coaches and schoolteachers. My phone was on fire. A lot of the messages reminded me that I'd said in the past how I wanted to become the best player in the world. It was massive for me to hear that and a reminder of the journey I'd been on to that point. One of the messages was from my old sevens coach, James Bailey. He remembered me telling him my long-term goals, one of which came true in Monaco. When I was at Hartpury College, I was in and out of the England set-up. I was part of an England development team that played sevens. I was too young to play matches initially, but I could train. It was then that the fire really started to burn brightly in me. I played my first couple of seasons with England, and then I had to choose between sevens and 15s rugby. At the time, I set some pretty big goals.

I wanted to be the best player in the world. I wanted to be an Olympian. And I wanted to be a World Cup winner. It was quite specific, but I actually set out that I wanted to be 24 or 25 by the time I got world player of the year. I thought that if I reached that goal while I was still young, I could use the achievement to take rugby and the women's game to a place it's never been. What I didn't want was to win such an award right at the end of my career, and for it to be seen as the pinnacle, or the moment when I bowed out of rugby. James reminded me of that.

I'd had a phenomenal year, but I believe that I'll put myself into contention for winning the World Rugby award again. At the same time, I'm not sure I ever want to feel like I'm at the top of my game, because it would also mean there was no room for improvement. That's something I will always continue to strive for. I'm still in the middle of my career and there's so much more I want to do. But the Monaco award made me realise it's important to celebrate and recognise achievements and milestones when they happen along the way. Monaco was a really proud moment for me and my family and a brilliant end to 2024.

CHAPTER 9

But as I relaxed back at home in Yorkshire that Christmas, I knew the start of 2025 was around the corner and that only meant one thing. It was the year we'd all been waiting for.

It was World Cup time.

10
Lukewarm Is No Good

I've always had a really close relationship with my mum. She understands me better than anyone. One day, during my teenage years, she sent me a print of a quote she thought would resonate with me. It read: 'Lukewarm is no good.' I had the print framed. I also had it saved as my phone background for a long time, and it is still at the top of the biographies on my Instagram and X pages. The full quote, which is taken from the legendary author Roald Dahl's 1979 novel *My Uncle Oswald*, reads as follows:

> I began to realise how important it was to be an enthusiast in life. If you are interested in something, no matter what it is, go at it at full speed ahead. Embrace it with both arms, hug it, love it and above all become passionate about it. Lukewarm is no good. Hot is no good either. White hot and passionate is the only thing to be.

It is the last three sentences that really hit home with me. They jumped off the page and punched me square in the face when I read them for the first time, because I think they perfectly sum

CHAPTER 10

up my mindset and approach to life. My mum was right. I've always been someone who is white hot. I've never been lukewarm at anything. I jump in at the deep end. I get asked quite often how I've got to the point I am in life, and what makes me tick. It's a difficult question. The answer is complex. But if I was asked to find a response in four words, then I would go back to Dahl every time. Lukewarm is no good. It's not a phrase I can claim to have come up with myself, but it's one I live by on a daily basis. Fortunately, I don't have to try too hard because being white hot and passionate about anything I do comes entirely naturally to me. I appreciate other people are wired differently. But to me, life is all about doing as Dahl says.

There should never be any holding back. No matter what situation you find yourself in – whether it's your relationship, friendships, business, career or sport – my view is that you'll never make that thing as good as it can be if you're lukewarm about it. Only by committing to something 100 per cent – or, in Dahl's words, by being white hot – can you reach your full potential. Imagine a tap with lukewarm water running out of it. It's a nice, comfortable temperature and you can keep your arm under it for ages and ages until it starts to ache. Nothing really changes. But if either boiling hot or freezing cold water comes out of that tap, your hand can only stay under it for a second or two before your body makes it pull away. It creates a reaction. It creates change. That's how I approach everything I do. I'm never at 50 per cent. Whatever it is, I'm all in.

If you're struggling to find the drive to do something – whatever it is – then I would say you're not doing the right thing for you. Rugby has always been the one constant in my life and the thing I've been most passionate about since my first days playing at Keighley Albion. But my lukewarm-is-no-good approach also applies to anything else I do, like when I tried to become a piano player. I loved piano and fully threw myself into trying to learn to play it. Eventually, I realised I was kind of s*** at it, but by committing 100 per cent I was able to find that out, then move on. I wouldn't have known that so quickly if I'd just said to myself: 'Oh you know what, maybe I'll do piano every now and again.' The same thing happened when I tried to learn the guitar.

It's natural that certain things aren't for certain people. Neither piano nor the guitar were for me. I wasn't born good at rugby. At times, I dropped the ball. I wasn't always successful and had to overcome obstacles. But I was white hot about my rugby. That's never left me. It's always been my main driver, and I've pushed through the hard times.

The rugby side of my life provides a lot of structure and routine, but I would describe my day-to-day life as chaotic. There is no consistency to it outside of my schedule with Harlequins and England. I know weeks in advance what time I've got to arrive at training and matches, what time they will finish. I know what I need to do in the gym or on the rugby field, and what I have to eat and when. That is the very definition of organisation. But away from the structure of being a professional rugby player, I am surrounded by chaos. In other areas of my life, there are some days when I have no idea what is happening.

Part of that is because I am now so busy with all sorts of different ventures away from professional sport. But the main

CHAPTER 10

reason is that it's just the way I'm wired. I love being able to feel free in every single aspect of my existence. I remember my mum saying to me once that I was born to run, and I still feel like that today. In many ways, my life has the same characteristics on and off the field. In rugby, I like to play off the cuff and let instinct take over. I think that's why I love playing full-back, because when you collect the ball in the back field, you have so many different opportunities in front of you. You can run, pass or kick. All manner of options can present themselves and you have the freedom to choose what you think is the right one.

Away from rugby, in any given week I might be doing a sponsorship appearance, a podcast, a fashion shoot or a media interview, or maybe snatching time for myself here and there. And the same freedom and spontaneity applies.

For instance, last Christmas, I went into Reading to visit the nail salon. I hadn't got an appointment, so I asked the man how long the wait was. The answer was 40 minutes. I could have sat down, grabbed a coffee and just waited patiently. It would have been a perfect time to relax – something which is pretty rare these days. But that's not how my brain works. Here was an unexpected opportunity to go round a few of the shops and get some more Christmas presents. When I got back to the salon, I'd missed my slot but was told they had another in 10 minutes' time. I decided to drive back home and drop off the presents. I got back about 15 minutes later, and I'd missed my slot again. It was going to be another 10 minutes. This time it felt natural to wait. I know it wasn't the most efficient use of time, but I would never find that frustrating. I feel very comfortable living moment to moment, in what some might see as chaos. It feels free to me.

Another example is packing. My teammates have told me to pack the night before I'm travelling the next morning for training or a game, especially if we have an early start. Not me. I don't understand how people can do it. I have tried. But as soon as I wake up, I start to overthink things. I worry about whether I've packed certain items and have to double check. Then I start thinking: 'Maybe I could wear this instead of that? My white top would go better with those jeans.' All I do is unpack the bag and start again.

Fortunately, with Harlequins and England the only things you really need to bring in your bag from home are your boots and gumshield. That's because all your warm-up and match kit is waiting for you at the ground. I've worked out that if I have too much time to do things, it just gives me leeway to completely change my mind, so I pack my bag about 15 minutes before leaving home for a match. But that's not a perfect system, either.

I remember one game when I was at Wasps, and we were travelling to Sale. We went on a team bus, which was unusual. I almost always travel by car, and that has all the gear I need in it, so it's the safer option. But that day, we met up and got a team bus to the north. We were going up the M1 when I had a sinking feeling that something was wrong. All of a sudden, I realised what it was: 'S***! I've forgotten my boots!' It was too late to turn back, so I had to wear our coach Giselle Mather's boots instead. They were these gold, ancient things, but they

CHAPTER 10

fitted well enough and so I cracked on. I got player of the match in that game. Things always tend to work out okay.

I also managed to turn up to a Harlequins game last season with two left boots, which was pretty impressive. I only realised when I tried to put them on for the warm-up. One of my teammates who wasn't playing that day had her boots in the back of her car, so I borrowed them. They were a little bit small, but good enough to play in. I scored a couple of tries that day and played well, so again, all was fine in the end. These sorts of incidents probably give me a false sense of security that things will never ever go really wrong, but that is how I approach each day.

Losing or forgetting things is part of my life. I used to have a keyring with both my car and house keys on it, then I lost it. So now when I go out I have to take my spare car key with me, and leave my remaining house key in a lockbox outside my front door. That means that if I lose my car key, at least I can get into my home. If I had to remember my match shirt, I'd probably lose that as well. To be honest, I'd probably lose my head if it wasn't screwed on.

Harlequins training doesn't finish until late in the evening. I might not get home until 10pm or so, and since I can't just go straight to sleep I'm often awake until midnight. But I also need to sleep to prioritise my recovery. That sometimes makes early mornings difficult. I realised I was snoozing my alarm too often, so, as a way of bringing structure to my mornings, I've taken to ordering a takeaway coffee to come to my front door. The time varies depending on what I'm up to that day, but I go for a flat white. I've found it's a good way of establishing a solid routine. Ordering the coffee the night before means that I know the doorbell is going to ring the next morning. It leaves me no choice other than to get up, and then I can crack on with my day. It's not the drink itself that I like the most: I don't order it for the caffeine hit; I don't have coffee in the house and could easily have a decaf instead. It's what it brings to the start of my days. When I was first with England sevens, I didn't actually like coffee at all. I'd order a hot chocolate in coffee shops, but I just looked like a big kid doing that. Eventually, I started trying a mocha, and now I'm on the flat whites. Maybe it's a sign I'm slowly growing up at last ...

Just like me, my hair is also naturally chaotic. It's not straight hair. It's loud and in your face, and I like that. Even if you know nothing about me, it's probably one of the first things you recognise. It's a big part of my life and I definitely see it as one of my superpowers. I do my hair in a number of different ways. Sometimes it's braided or plaited. But these days, more often than not I play with my hair down. Having big, curly hair on the field looks different and stands out. If people watch a game in which I play, they might not have any idea who I am. If I don't score a try, they might not remember me or the way I played. I hope that doesn't happen, but as a last resort they might remember me for my hair.

But having my hair down isn't all about what others think. There is a very personal reason why I've started to do it more often. It might sound odd, but I feel it's really brought my game on. Having my hair loose gives me a lot of confidence. As I've got a bit older and looked after it more, my hair has got bigger

CHAPTER 10

and bigger. When I went through a period of eating poorly and losing a lot of weight, I really struggled for body confidence. I'd wear shoulder pads to try and make myself look bigger, but I would still lose the physical battles in both attack and defence. In contact, I'd have the ball stripped from me too easily.

But in one game during that period I played with my hair loose and it gave me back a bit of the confidence I'd lost. It felt like a turning point, so I've stayed with it.

With big curly hair, I feel I have more of a presence on the field. Rugby is obviously a hugely physical sport, but I think it's got a big mindset element to it, too. If you're in a good place mentally, if you believe in yourself and you're confident in what you do, you can always make an impact. When I make a tackle with my hair out, it flings forward in the contact because it's so big. When I get up, the movement in my hair makes me think: 'S***. I smashed that person. My God, now I've got the confidence to go smash someone else.'

The reality might be entirely different and I might not have smashed the opposition player at all. But that's how it makes me feel. Having my hair out gives me a presence I don't have when it's tied up. It makes me feel more comfortable on the field. Now, getting my hair right is by far the most important aspect of my pre-game routine. I wash it on the morning of the match. Before I started wearing my hair loose, I'd braided it for ages. Lots of women's rugby players do that, or put their hair in plaits, mainly to avoid getting it pulled in tackles. I do still get my head braided every now and again, especially if it's raining, or if I'm going to be getting in and out of water all the time, like when I'm on holiday. In those scenarios, it's just easier and means I have one less thing to think about. My hair doesn't tend to work too well in the rain. Weirdly, I haven't actually played many of my England matches in wet weather. But the 2024 Six Nations game away to Scotland was one. We did the warm-up and then, when we lined up for the national anthems, the heavens opened. I'd never seen rain quite like it. I'd worn my hair down, and though in my I head I looked like Angelina Jolie, I actually ended up looking like a wet dog. When I saw myself on the big screen I couldn't believe my appearance. Jess Breach came up to me and said: 'I love you to bits, Ellie, but please put your hair up!'

Fashion, photography and music are three of my biggest passions away from rugby. I loved doing art at school. It first started when I painted the penny at East Morton. I've always loved fashion too. Growing up, I didn't really feel comfortable in a lot of the clothes I was wearing. I think that's because, being a female athlete, I was always bigger than my friends that weren't playing high-level sport. I'd try and hide my body and muscles by wearing dresses with long sleeves or a high or turtleneck top. For a long time, I couldn't find a style that I was confident in. Eventually, though, I did and it's allowed me to feel more comfortable and express who I am as a person through the clothes I wear.

As a rugby player, you're essentially in uniform all the time, wearing the kit provided for training and matches. So, in my day-to-day life, I want to put personality into how I look. I like looking nice and feeling confident, and I like to share

CHAPTER 10

my outfits on social media. I've got a section on my Instagram page devoted solely to that. I avoid mainstream shops on the high street. Instead, I go looking for independent or thrift shops, where you can buy clothes no one else has. It's one of my favourite things to do when I have the time.

I love to use my clothes to help me be different and stand out from the crowd. My worst nightmare would be turning up to a function wearing the same thing as someone else. I absolutely hate the thought of that. I'll wear outfits like massive basketball shorts with a little top. On one occasion, when I was in New Zealand, I bought a couple of professional cycling tops and I wore them out to dinner with big, baggy trousers. It was a very weird combination, don't get me wrong. But I thought it looked really cool. Most importantly, I knew no one else would be wearing it.

The reason I've always loved photography is because every year for as long as I can remember, my mum has made me a picture book for Christmas. When we were growing up, she'd always be making home videos and taking photos to document our lives. I love looking back on those memories, especially when I go back home to Riddlesden, so it's something I've made part of my life too. Even when I was really young I'd help my mum with her marketing campaigns. After working for Bradford & Bingley, she moved on to Hallmark Cards. On one occasion, I helped her with a promotional video for the company, working on the voiceover and filming. She always asked my opinion, and I think I learned a lot on those projects.

My photography really stepped up in New Zealand at the 2022 World Cup. I took an old-school film camera out with me and would take pictures wherever we went. I prefer vintage to modern fashion and it's the same with photography. Sometimes when I'm in camp with England, I like to use a disposable camera. Film is expensive to develop these days, but those pictures provide a different sort of energy to the ones you get from a digital camera. Someone once told me that they could recognise the pictures I posted on Instagram without needing to see my name next to them, because they have a certain feel. I loved hearing that.

The creative outlets I enjoy – like fashion and photography – enhance my life. I firmly believe that doing them makes me a better player. They allow me to properly switch off from rugby, which is really important.

I want to be the best player I can be, firstly because I want to be able to end my career knowing I gave it everything. But I also want to inspire people. I want to show people that if they're stuck on something or struggling for motivation, there's always another 1 per cent you can put in. That approach has always been natural to me. I've always wanted to improve in every aspect of my life, and I want to pass that mindset on to others. In the end, it all comes back to Dahl. As he says, lukewarm is no good. Hot is no good either. White hot and passionate is the only thing to be. Remember that and, in my view, I don't think you can go too far wrong.

11
ADHD

By the time 2025 arrived, with a home World Cup on the horizon, I knew I was set for the biggest year of my career so far. On the field, my game was in a good place. On the whole, things were good away from rugby, too, but I wanted to make sure I was in the best place possible to perform. We won the WXV tournament in Canada at the end of 2024, and after we came back I was struggling to sleep because my brain just wouldn't switch off. I couldn't stop countless thoughts going round and round in my head. It meant I wasn't nodding off until the early hours of the morning, which wasn't great for my preparation and recovery.

In training and meetings, I began to realise I was struggling to fully understand what other people were saying, and also to get my views across. And I was still as disorganised as ever.

I was aware that these things were stopping me from becoming the best player I could be, so I went to see the England team doctor, who sent me for a referral to try and get to the bottom of some of the things I was experiencing. I had to go through a long process of questionnaires and tests as well as speaking to a psychiatrist. It was a very rigorous process and the tests were

CHAPTER 11

far from easy. My mum and dad and even my old schoolteachers also provided input. One of the tests was the dullest thing I've ever done in my life. It was an hour long, broken down into three 20-minute segments. Different colours would appear on a screen and, depending on which colour came up, you had to press a certain arrow. During the last 20 minutes, I just kept clicking the same arrow every single time because I got so bored.

One of the things that came out of the evaluation was that while I had done well at school, there were consistent themes to my reports. I would always get notes observing that I talked all the time and distracted others. I was regularly told I needed to focus more. In the end, after all the results came back, I was told I had Attention-Deficit/Hyperactivity Disorder, which is more commonly known as ADHD. It is defined as:

> A neurodevelopmental condition characterised by persistent patterns of inattention, hyperactivity and impulsivity that interfere with daily functioning and development, often starting in childhood and continuing into adulthood. People with ADHD may struggle to focus, sit still, or control impulses. But the presentation varies, with some primarily experiencing inattention, others hyperactivity or impulsivity, and some a combination of both.

More detailed symptoms of ADHD include:

Inattention: Difficulty focusing, organising tasks, staying on track, listening and often losing things.

With the family (from left to right: dad Nigel, brother Sam and mum Alison), after my England debut against Canada in November 2017. I marked my bow with a try.

I was player of the match against Ireland in the 2018 Six Nations in Coventry. I had plenty of friends and family there watching to celebrate the achievement with!

European sevens champions with England at under-18 level. That tournament was held in Vichy, France.

Ahead of the 2024 Olympics, my brother Sam and I both represented Great Britain at a sevens tournament in Hamburg, Germany. It was a special moment for our family.

Relaxing away from rugby is incredibly important but I do like to keep busy when I'm not training or playing. Sometimes that includes being upside down!

My brother Sam has also carved out a career in rugby and is currently playing for Ampthill in the RFU Champ.

I didn't make it to the Tokyo Olympics, so to represent Great Britain in rugby sevens at the Paris Games of 2024 fulfilled a lifelong ambition.

I absolutely loved everything about Paris, even though as a Great Britain side we didn't manage to win a medal.

I had an eventful journey to Monaco for the 2024 World Rugby awards when my plane was cancelled, but we made it eventually.

Women's World Player of the Year for 2024. An incredible honour and privilege. It's an award I want to win again one day.

All smiles with my mum after being named the best women's player on the planet – something I never thought I'd achieve.

Banging the drum for my England team-mates while on the sidelines at the 2025 World Cup.

Walking out at Cardiff's Principality Stadium for my 50th England cap against Wales. I marked the milestone with a hat-trick.

Inspiring the next generation of rugby players – both male and female – is a big part of why I play the game. Representing England is a chance to do just that.

I'm fortunate to be part of an England team that is used to winning. We've won the past four Women's Six Nations titles with a Grand Slam.

Lifting the 2025 Women's World Cup after the final victory over Canada at a sold-out Allianz Stadium was the culmination of a lifelong dream.

Celebrating the moment we'd all been waiting for with my parents.

Sharing my milestones with those closest to me makes my achievements even more special.

Me? A Barbie? Playing professional rugby has thrown up some incredible opportunities but I never thought I'd be made into a doll! Even the hair and nose ring were spot on!

I was shocked to be nominated for the 2025 BBC Sports Personality of the Year award. To finish as runner-up was beyond my wildest dreams.

At the start of 2026, we celebrated our World Cup win with visits to Windsor Castle and No. 10. The Princess of Wales has been one of our biggest and most high-profile supporters.

Appearing on *The Jonathan Ross Show* alongside the likes of Hugh Bonneville and Jason Derulo was a surreal moment. The knocks to my knees told the audience I was a rugby player if they weren't sure before!

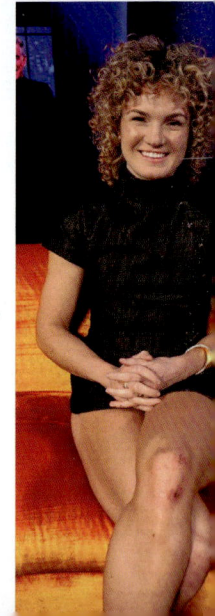

Hyperactivity: Fidgeting, excessive movement, trouble staying seated, feeling restless and talking excessively.

Impulsivity: Acting without thinking, blurting out answers, interrupting others and difficulty waiting for their turn.

I tick a lot of those boxes. I was prescribed medication, which I took for a couple of months, but then I came off it ahead of the 2025 Six Nations. The medication had its side effects. I was told it could cause depression, among other things, and it could also suppress your appetite. It means you've got to be careful about finding the right dosage. If you don't, it can do you more harm than good. It's also not as simple as just taking a tablet and expecting everything to change overnight.

As I mentioned in the previous chapter, the way I live my life is very hyperactive and impulsive. My brain is always going at 100 miles an hour. I like chaos; that's just the way I'm wired. The ADHD medication slowed those thoughts down, which is what it is designed to do. All of a sudden, my head went from being loud to very, very quiet. All was still.

I hated that feeling. It made me feel incredibly lonely. I wouldn't necessarily say I was depressed, but I did feel down. I don't know whether that was purely due to the medication I'd started taking, or to other aspects of my life. What I did know was that the medication wasn't for me. That's not to say I wouldn't go back on it in the future, if I felt it was the right decision. But I wanted to be happy and enjoy my rugby. That was the most important thing for me. So, when I found

CHAPTER 11

that the medication stopped me doing that, I decided to move on from it.

Being told I had ADHD didn't necessarily change anything for me. It's not like it turned my life upside down. It's estimated that more than 2.5 million people in the United Kingdom are in the same boat as me, so I'm far from alone. What it did do was give me a better understanding of myself.

When I was at school, I often wondered why I wasn't able to concentrate as well as the other children in the class. I wondered why I'd want to talk to other pupils all the time and why I couldn't just sit still and be quiet. Now I know that ADHD was at least partly responsible. That doesn't pardon me of anything. It's not about creating excuses.

I've always had the same trouble listening in team meetings as I did listening in school. That's because I have difficulty focusing in that kind of environment. My timekeeping hasn't always been perfect, either. But now I understand myself better, I try to fight against the urge to leave everything to the last minute. I know what's going on inside my brain, so I do my best to arrive on time. These days, if I have a question or a point to raise in a team meeting, I won't blurt it out to everyone in the room as soon as it enters my head. That's what I used to do.

Instead, I write down the question or point I want to make in my notepad and then speak at the end. These might seem like small things, but I think they've definitely helped with my communication. I'm still really honest with my feelings, both in rugby meetings and in my personal life. But I've worked hard to make sure I get what I need to say across in just a few words, rather than rambling, because that's no good, especially in a sporting environment.

Being told you have ADHD is often seen as a medical diagnosis. I don't like the word diagnosis in this context. In my opinion, it gives off a negative energy. ADHD is not an illness and it's not something that needs to hold you back. In fact, the opposite is true.

I use my ADHD as a superpower. Having a greater understanding of how my brain works has given me the chance to find a way of living and playing that allows me to be at my best. It takes time to get a strategy in place, but for me ADHD is a blessing not a curse. For whatever reason, my brain has been made to run quicker than normal. I'm creative and I think in a different way. So, my view is it would be madness not to try and use that to my advantage. If I'm not able to sleep because I'm thinking of a certain rugby move I want to practise in training, then instead of worrying about the fact I should be resting, I see that as a strength. As long as I write those thoughts down and actually use them when I get to training the next day, then I look at that as a positive not a negative.

ADHD presents itself differently in different people, so not everyone will experience the same things I do. But the overriding thing I would say is that ADHD should be seen as something to help you push forward in life, not hold you back. It's certainly helped me a lot and continues to do so.

Looking back to the time I was injured with England sevens, I can see now that it was my ADHD which allowed me to hyper focus on working out how long it took for my teammates to

CHAPTER 11

catch and pass the ball. My attention to minute details like that, when I'm super engaged, helps me to be a better player and improves us as a team. If that's the case, why not embrace it?

It's not just me who's benefited from knowing about my ADHD. It's allowed my family, friends and teammates to understand me better as well. Since being told about my ADHD, I've been my authentic self far more often. In the past, some of my behaviours have led to me being labelled as a people pleaser or an attention seeker. Now, others can see why I am who I am. In turn, that's made me feel safer and more at peace with myself. I also believe it's allowed me to blossom both as a player and a person. I've always known who I am, but the times when I've been misunderstood in the past have left me questioning myself. I'm definitely happier for understanding why I am the way I am.

Although I'd worked hard to move on from the issues I'd had with food and losing too much weight, before being told about my ADHD my diet could still have been better. I was so focused on improving my rugby that I'd sometimes forget the importance of eating. Again, I now understand part of the reason for that is ADHD and how my brain works. It's not the case that I don't want to eat. What happens in my head is that if I'm focused fully on something else – whether it's rugby or photography, or anything really – I totally prioritise that thing. In such a scenario, my brain has no space for anything else, and I can forget about eating altogether.

My food intake is something I now keep an eye on all the time. Emily Ross, the England physio, has been a huge help to me across my career. She was the first person I opened up to about my problems with food, when she came down to Wasps, so she knows exactly what I've been through. On England camps, she'll occasionally sit down with me to check in on my diet. It might be when I'm on the physio bed getting a massage or some treatment, or in our downtime. Whenever we can get a moment together, really. If I don't think my eating is going well, then I will tell Emily and we can put a plan in place to make changes. On the whole, though, that hasn't been the case.

Emily has played a fundamental role in me getting to the place where I am now. But I've also spoken to my teammates at both club and country about the position I was in with food. They always have a little eye on me, too. I don't have a problem with food now. I'm never trying to lose weight and I'm certainly not trying to look small, like I did in the past. But a busy life and my ADHD means I really have to focus on eating the right things at the right time. All those supermarket meal deals I was eating when I was at Wasps and travelling a lot are a good example. I don't really like having sandwiches now as a result, which is a good thing as they aren't a healthy choice.

My ADHD also means that I can get overstimulated when I'm in a team environment and, when that happens, it can make me feel sick and nauseous. That can put me off my food, especially if I'm in a busy room with a lot of people.

My friends now recognise that. They'll say to me: 'Ellie, shall we go and sit on another table that's a bit quieter?' Or: 'Maybe you should just come down in five minutes when it's less busy.' That's what I mean when I say that being told I have

CHAPTER 11

ADHD hasn't just helped me. It's also allowed others to work out why I am the way I am. The benefits have been multifaceted.

I had never actually planned to talk openly about ADHD. When I went through the tests and was told I had it, I was initially going to keep it to myself. I didn't want people to create excuses for me. But I'm so glad I did because I believe I'm happier for doing so. And if talking about it can also help others, then that can only be a good thing. There is a lot more awareness in society now about ADHD and how it affects people's lives. Again, that's a big benefit.

I don't think my mum or dad really believed in ADHD at first. But after being involved in the process of the tests, I've definitely seen a difference in the ways they help and support me. If I'm on the phone to my mum, she'll throw into our conversation at the end: 'Ellie, make sure you eat.'

One of the things I'm not very good at is sorting out my car. A few months ago, when I was back at home, I had to take my old vehicle in for a part to be changed. I kept putting it off because I just didn't want to do it. I delay boring jobs like that as long as possible. Because my dad now has a better understanding of me as a person with ADHD, he told me he'd sort out the issue for me, which I was very grateful for. It's not about getting other people to do things for me, though. Instead, it's about having a support system around me, with people who understand that I find some things easy and others more difficult.

I've made a lot of strides since being told about my ADHD. I've spoken with the people who run Harlequins and discussed how we can make our team meetings as effective as they can be for everyone. Sometimes, when coaches explain tactics in a certain way, I just can't get my head around it and might need to be told using a different approach. Again, my coaches and teammates now understand why. The way I respond best to the coaches is by receiving clear and concise information, focused on one or two key points. If I'm told lots and lots of different things at once, I struggle to process it all and nothing sinks in.

And if things don't go well in training and we make a lot of mistakes, I often get very frustrated. The girls at England call me 'Kevin', after the character in the film *Kevin & Perry Go Large*, because I get angry if, for example, there are too many dropped balls or a particular move isn't working well. 'Kevin' is my moody alter ego, but the girls now know I'll return to Ellie soon enough.

Don't get me wrong, being told I have ADHD hasn't made me a totally different person. I still struggle with lots of things; though I don't think I needed 'fixing' anyway. ADHD is a part of who I am and I don't want that to change. I still put too many things off. I'm still really bad at texting back. Meg Jones, my England teammate, takes the mick out of me for that all the time. I'm not ignoring people's messages. I'm not being rude. I'm aware I need to reply. It's that just at certain times my brain is so full that I physically can't reply. This happens more often now that my phone is a lot busier. The same applies to my emails. I miss them all the time, mainly because I have tens of thousands of unread messages. Most of them are spam, or from shopping I've been doing. I get totally overwhelmed by the number and say to myself: 'I'll find that email tomorrow.' But when tomorrow comes, do I find that email?

CHAPTER 11

The one ADHD presentation I will always love to tap into is the creative side of my brain. I don't ever want that part of me to change. In the last year or so, my mum and dad have said to me: 'Ellie, you need to slow down. Why don't you just sit down and watch something on TV?'

Sitting on the sofa watching a film is a way they can relax, because they don't have ADHD. It does not work for me. I might put the TV on, and have one eye on it, but I'll also be doing something else at the same time – like editing pictures I've taken. I always need to have things to work on away from rugby, or I get really frustrated with myself and feel like I'm wasting time.

Photography and fashion provide a creative outlet that allows me to relax. I remember one sevens tournament I went to in Madrid, before the Paris Olympics. Between our matches, my teammates would use the breaks to take a rest. Some would use recovery methods, such as ice baths or compression pumps for their legs. Others would even fall asleep. I cannot just sit down and do nothing. So, I went around the stadium taking pictures of the fans. That was my way of recharging. I wouldn't change it for the world.

ADHD is now officially a part of my make-up, but it doesn't change who I am.

12

World Cup

18
World Cup

As a Red Roses team, we'd known since May 2022 that England would host the 2025 Women's World Cup. We'd spent so long talking about it that the start of the year almost came as a bit of a relief. It had been creeping up on us. Now, all of a sudden, it was here. As a team, we couldn't rest on our laurels. But there was no danger of that, not with the competitiveness of our squad and Mitch as our coach. And, as a player, I knew I had to keep on pushing to get better and better so that I could ensure I got the game time I needed to put myself in the best place to make the World Cup squad. There was absolutely no guarantee of selection.

The first few months of 2025 made the imminent World Cup feel very real. But it also came with worry, because we all knew that if injury struck at any point it could potentially ruin our tournament hopes. I try not to think about negatives like that. It's not helpful. I was just determined to focus on where I could improve on the field. I learn so much from playing games, potentially more than from training. So, match minutes are really important to me. I went into the 2025 Six Nations excited about what was to come. And then, out of nowhere,

CHAPTER 12

injury struck – a grade-three hamstring tear. Hamstring injuries are ranked numerically in terms of severity. So, while it could have been worse, it really scared me for a couple of reasons. The first because I was so surprised by it. The second and more obvious reason was that with the World Cup around the corner, it immediately gave me very real fitness concerns.

The injury happened against Scotland. I'd come off the bench for the 38-5 win over Italy in York and then marked my 50th cap with a hat-trick against Wales. We won 67-12 in Cardiff, with my good friend Abi Burton also scoring twice on her debut. I roomed with Abi, who I've known well since my days at Hartpury, ahead of that game, and was delighted for her. It was a great way for me to celebrate a milestone game before, in round three, we beat Ireland 49-5 in Cork. The Championship was going to plan for us. Then, in round four, calamity hit. I played the full 80 minutes of the 59-7 home victory over Scotland, played in Leicester and that was the odd thing. My hamstring didn't hurt at all. I didn't get substituted because I didn't realise I'd been injured. I was still performing well and didn't feel anything out of the ordinary. The hamstring did feel a little bit tight at the end of the game – which is something that's not unusual – and at full time I reported that to the coaching staff in the Welford Road changing room. I had a scan, but even at that point I wasn't worried. Then the results came back and my emotions changed completely.

I was told the scan results showed I'd suffered a worrying injury. This was obviously a huge shock. I had to process the news that I'd not only miss another Grand Slam decider with France, but also face a period of time on the sidelines. I was told I would be out of action for a few weeks, though with hamstring injuries you can never be quite sure. The injury just came out of nowhere. There was no warning. I was well aware that I had been playing a lot of rugby. In 2024, I'd taken part in the Six Nations and then gone to the Olympics in Paris. I hadn't really had a break, but it had been a good year, and I just wanted to keep on improving and pushing for that World Cup spot. I was still hitting personal bests in the gym, for both strength and speed. My GPS numbers were higher than ever. In the run-up to the Scotland game, my body felt close to, if not the best it ever had been. But at the same time, your body also has a weird way of telling you when you're getting to breaking point. The hamstring injury, I think, was my body's way of doing exactly that.

Looking back now, I can see that I was mentally tired without knowing it. Something needed to give and that something just happened to be my hamstring. I didn't actually feel like I needed a mental break. But my body decided for me. When something like that happens, you can't control it. You have no other choice than to accept it and move on by working hard to get back to full fitness as soon as possible. I cheered myself up with the notion that everything happens for a reason.

While I was a child at East Morton, I went to Sunday school, and the whole family attended church regularly. When we were growing up, we'd never be allowed to say things like 'Oh my God' or 'Jesus' in the house. Now, though, I don't believe in God, and I wouldn't consider myself religious at all. But I do believe

CHAPTER 12

there is something or somebody out there looking over us, and that they wanted to challenge me in a different way. I had been looking forward to some time off after that Six Nations and before the start of the World Cup preparation training camps. But that being, or whatever it is they are, said: 'No, you can't do that yet. We want you to keep working hard for now.' And so that is what I did.

The first game I would miss was France at home. I know that with the World Cup approaching, some people were worried about my injury. I did really, really want to play against France and was gutted to miss out. Everyone wants to play a Grand Slam decider, especially at Allianz Stadium. And, aside from my own desires, I also knew people wanted to watch me play. But I had full faith in Emma Sing, who started at full-back against France. I knew that with her talent and skills she'd put the team in the best place possible. I knew my teammates would do the job without me. I was just jealous I wasn't on the pitch, especially as there was another big crowd of 37,573 cheering us on. I was at Allianz Stadium for the tense game, which we won by a point, 43-42. Emma scored two tries, and with England 31-7 up at the end of the first half, the game looked to be in the bag. I watched from the stands as France mounted a mammoth comeback after the break. There were a few nerves at times, but the team held on by the narrowest of margins. It was our fourth successive Grand Slam and the perfect World Cup preparation.

Most of the girls went away on holiday after that to enjoy some well-deserved downtime. But after resting my hamstring for a little bit, my work was only just getting started. As a professional sportswoman, you can never be certain what you're going to be doing in the summer. I was supposed to be going away with my mum and dad at some point. But I'd not actually booked a holiday. I was so focused on rugby during the Six Nations that the rest of my life became secondary. And, of course, there was my general disorganisation. So there was nothing to cancel once I knew my plans had changed due to the hamstring injury. My friends sometimes criticise me for being a bit chaotic, but it can have its benefits.

For me, it was all about a total switch of mindset. I'd expected May and June to be a quiet period, and a chance to switch off from rugby. Now, with an injury to manage and recover from, I knew there was only one thing to do and that was work very hard. The message was clear. The No. 1 aim, of course, was to get my hamstring healed. There was a lot of bike work and treatment on the physio bed, but luckily I did not need an operation. I spent most of May at Pennyhill Park, which is England Rugby's high-performance base. Emily Ross was my main physio and stayed with me through the rehabilitation process. Emily had previous for working miracles ahead of World Cups. Before the 2022 tournament in New Zealand, she helped Abby Dow recover from a broken leg in time to play. My injury was clearly nowhere near as serious as Abby's. But, still, I wouldn't have been able to complete the recovery process without Emily. Her dedication is just incredible. She would spend long, long hours with me at Pennyhill – sometimes even whole days – helping to massage and heal my hamstring. Once I could

CHAPTER 12

start cycling on a static bike again to get my legs moving, Emily got a bike of her own and cycled next to me just to keep me company. Our sessions would vary in length, but Emily would often cycle next to me for half an hour or more. Talk about going above and beyond. It definitely felt like we were part of a team, and her company made a big difference to me. That summer was particularly hot, so we'd often put the static bikes outside to cycle in the sun. I was never going to be short of motivation to recover with a home World Cup around the corner, but Emily pushed me on. I'm fortunate to have worked with her for a few years now. Emily knows me personally as much as she does physically and was a huge help to me with the problems I experienced with food. Having that personal relationship makes a big difference. She's been there for me constantly, whatever I need. Not only does she know which buttons to push to get me going, she also probably understands my body better than I do. The time we spent together just brought us even closer, if that were possible. You've got to trust your physios. You spend a lot of time with them, but there was no better person to look after me. After getting down to work on my rehabilitation and being given reassurances by Emily, I was confident I'd be good to go for the World Cup.

Mitch had appointed Zoe Stratford as captain for the 2025 Six Nations. Zoe took over from Marlie Packer. In the media, it was seen as a shock move by Mitch, because Marlie had been captain since 2023, when Sarah Hunter retired. One of the other things Mitch had done when he became coach was to bring Natasha 'Mo' Hunt back into the team. She'd been left out of the 2022 World Cup tournament, but by 2025 she was the No. 1 scrum-half. Outside of the camp, Zoe succeeding Marlie as skipper was seen as a big thing – a way of Mitch keeping the squad on its toes. I can only speak from personal experience, but it never felt as if that was a shock for the players. For me, nothing changed. I've always trusted the decisions of my coaches, and our England team has so many leaders, anyway. Zoe was one of those. As far as I was concerned, it didn't really matter who was named captain or vice-captain. We had a squad packed with experience, which was one of our greatest strengths going into the World Cup.

Throughout the summer, the build-up to the World Cup was really gathering momentum. We trained a lot at Pennyhill, but also at Hazelwood – London Irish's old facility – and for the first time in the history of England women's rugby, we also travelled abroad, to Treviso in Italy, with funding from the RFU. The 30-degree July heat made it a brutal environment to train in. But that camp put us in a great place. No stone was left unturned. We trained initially with 42 players, all of us knowing that only 32 would make the final World Cup squad.

We all talked about what our journey to the final and hopefully winning the tournament would look like. We compared that journey to someone trying to reach the summit of Mount Everest. If a mountaineer attempts to get to the top of Everest in one go, they'll fail. For sure. Most probably, they'll die. Conquering Everest is about breaking it down into sections and ticking them off as you go. It's a case of hitting mini base camps along the way, taking things step by step. We knew that

CHAPTER 12

if we were to be successful on home soil, that's what our World Cup would look like. Mitch instilled the Everest concept into us all, emphasising we'd already ticked off certain base camps, like winning the Six Nations. There would be further base camps to follow, like topping our pool and then navigating the knock-out stages.

We were hugely inspired by the Lionesses, as we had been the last time we went to a World Cup. In the summer of 2025, in the European Championships in Switzerland, they were defending the trophy they'd secured back in 2022. They managed this, beating Spain on penalties in the final, with Chloe Kelly the hero once again. As someone who grew up playing a lot of football, I followed the tournament closely, and we all watched the matches in our team room. The way Sarina Wiegman's team delivered at the highest level, and dealt with the huge pressure they were under, were things the Red Roses could definitely learn from.

When we did interviews ahead of the World Cup, there were – understandably – a lot of questions about women's football and about us as an England rugby team trying to emulate that success. What the Lionesses have done for women's football and female sport in general has been revolutionary. They have really helped grow not just the game's profile as a whole, but also their own individual brands, which can only be a good thing. As a squad, it would have been stupid not to be inspired by that. If we could have a sliver of the impact in rugby that the Lionesses had on women's football, we could chalk that up as a success. That was our target – to win a major trophy like the Lionesses, and by doing so inspire the next generation of rugby-playing girls and boys.

A number of our girls wore Lionesses shirts, and it was great to see Esme Morgan, one of their players, sporting a Red Roses top. I'd met a few of the England football girls, such as Chloe Kelly, throughout the year's run-up to the World Cup. There was a common bond between both teams. It just felt like we'd all come together regardless of the shape of the ball we were playing with. Now, it was up to us to emulate the Lionesses' success.

In the summer before the World Cup, I finally graduated from St Mary's University with a 2:1 in sports and exercise science. St Mary's also awarded me an honorary PhD, alongside my undergraduate degree. My degree took me six years because I did it part time alongside my rugby. I didn't experience university like most students do. In the back of my mind it was always something that I had to do, but I only went to a handful of lectures in person. Almost all of my work was done online.

St Mary's were great, allowing me the time to do my work over a far longer period than most of my fellow learners. My workload varied, but I roughly had one university assessment to do each month. I was helped a great deal by a lecturer called Jade Salim. I wouldn't have been able to graduate from university without her. She was a sports psychology lecturer, but she essentially became my mentor. Jade was very clear about letting me know my deadlines and what I had coming up in terms of assignments. She also provided invaluable advice, which I needed because I wasn't at the university physically. The other person who really helped me with my degree was my mum.

CHAPTER 12

It's a running joke in our family that my mum got the degree, not me. Obviously, it was me who did all the work. But my mum was a great support in terms of offering advice on how to structure assignments and how to reference them. These are the sorts of things I'd have checked with my fellow students if I was a normal student. But doing my degree part time and remotely meant I had no frame of reference or others to talk to. I wouldn't have been able to graduate without Jade and my mum.

Initially, I wasn't sure if I was going to go to my graduation, because it took place in the run-up to the World Cup, which was my full focus. But I was glad I did because I wanted to make sure I got a picture in my cap and gown for my Instagram, to show people that it is possible to do a degree while being a professional athlete.

On 24 July, Mitch announced the final World Cup squad at Allianz Stadium. In terms of the number of media personnel that attended, it was the biggest press conference in the history of England Rugby, both men's and women's. It was huge for us, bringing home how much interest there was in the players, the team and the tournament as a whole. Yes, that brought pressure with it. But we were determined to embrace it. In my interviews that day, I said as much, while also emphasising that I was now back to full fitness. I also made clear how delighted I was to be selected given my hamstring injury and the strength of the squad. By that day, it felt natural for us to be where we were. The months of build-up were behind us. Before the tournament, a few of the girls had done a television advert for O2, who are one of the biggest sponsors of the England team, where they jumped out of a plane. I don't want to give any secrets away, but professional sportswomen are definitely not allowed to do things like that! The advert was made with the help of artificial intelligence. There's no way Mitch would have given the greenlight for that. That was one of the last bits of fun before the rugby started. But the fact it even took place at all was a reflection of how far the women's game has come.

We were going into a home World Cup as the No. 1 team in the world, and everyone expected us to win. That meant that all the players were under pressure. But that was nothing new. We'd been under similar pressure going into the previous World Cup in New Zealand. But, on a personal level, I was very aware I'd perhaps added to the pressure on me by signing sponsorship deals and appearing in campaigns before the tournament. One of the big campaigns I was involved in before the World Cup was with the Japanese beer brand, Asahi, who were one of the tournament's main sponsors. While I was aware of the expectations surrounding the team, personally I saw any pressure as a positive. The reason it existed was because the team had had a very good couple of years. I'd much rather have been in that position than people thinking we had no chance whatsoever.

Mitch's World Cup planning had been carried out to a tee. He had a no-excuse mentality. We couldn't have been more prepared. Our Pool A games were against USA, Samoa and Australia. Everyone in the squad knew their roles. The plan for who would play each game had been laid out to us in advance. Clearly, this was subject to change if there were injuries. But

CHAPTER 12

the point is that nothing was being left to chance. We had two World Cup warm-up matches, against Spain and France. We hammered Spain 97-7, but I was always going to miss that game and then play against France. I think some people were worried I hadn't quite recovered from my hamstring injury when I wasn't named in the squad for Spain, but that wasn't the case. Mitch wanted to look at other players for that game. I started the 40-6 away victory over France. That was one of the best Red Roses performances I've been a part of. It was a dominant performance against a very good team.

It took our winning streak to 27 matches, dating back to our last loss, which was the 2022 World Cup final defeat by New Zealand. The long run of success brought with it expectation, and a lot of outside noise. But Mitch's message to us as a squad was that such pressure was a privilege. He made it clear we had to embrace it, and we were determined to do so. The plan was to ignore all the distractions, and I think we did that very well. The squad was so focused.

Since the beginning of his reign, Mitch had given me freedom to be myself on the pitch, backing me to play what I saw in front of me. His faith had paid off and helped me take my game to a new level. But ahead of the World Cup, he had another message for me: 'You can't train in the zoo and expect to play in the jungle.' It's a mantra I've also seen used by Arsenal manager Mikel Arteta. What Mitch meant was that in order for both me and the England team as a whole to deliver under the utmost pressure of a home World Cup, we'd have to train so incredibly hard that we'd be ready for anything. That's exactly what we did.

By the time we got to Sunderland for the tournament-opening game with the USA, I was caught between two contrasting emotions. This was the moment we'd been waiting three years for and there was no doubt we were ready for it. But, at the same time, I knew that kick-off at the Stadium of Light would mark the beginning of the end of something we'd all looked forward to so much. As soon as the World Cup started, it would in a sense be over. That's not a negative outlook, it's just what happens in professional sport. Campaigns come and go and everything moves so quickly. So, I'd made sure to remind myself to enjoy whatever was to come. In fact, I made a written note of it. On a piece of pink paper, I wrote down the words: 'Win the World Cup. Be happy doing it.' They were words I'd regularly revisit throughout the tournament.

As a northern girl, I absolutely loved the fact we started the World Cup in Sunderland. England's men's side plays all its games at Allianz Stadium in Twickenham. That has also become our home for big matches, and it's where the 2025 final was held. But the Red Roses have played at grounds in almost every corner of the country. Doing so has been a vitally important part of growing the women's game, and I think you saw that in Sunderland, which is not a traditional rugby hotbed. It was a huge game for me, because all my family and friends were there. And the World Cup couldn't have got off to a better start. We scored 11 tries in a 69-7 victory in front of a crowd of 42,723. The attendance surpassed the highest in women's World Cup history, beating the 42,579 who watched our 2022 final defeat by New Zealand at Eden Park. It was a strong statement of

CHAPTER 12

intent, in terms of what we could deliver, both as a team and in the stands. To play in front of such a big crowd was momentous for us, although we knew that, all being well, more was to come. In that game we matched forward power with some brilliant running rugby. I was fortunate enough to score two of our 11 tries, marking them with the 'cowboy' celebration which had become common by then.

The origins of the celebration began on a trip to Zante before Covid, when as a group of girls we said to each other: 'Shall we just be cowboys and have fun?' Then, when we were in New Zealand for the WXV tournament in late 2023, Jess Breach, Meg Jones and I dubbed ourselves 'The Cowboys' again. Meg was 'The Sheriff' because she's always in charge. It was just something random we came up with. When we found ourselves with some spare time on our hands, we thought it would be cool to use it to come up with a distinctive try celebration or dance routine. That was where the 'cowboy' celebration was born. One hand goes on the hip while the other is hoisted above the head and swung around in a lassoing motion. We also simultaneously bob from side to side, as though we are riding a horse.

Through 2024, cowboy hats quickly became a common sight at England matches, and it was amazing to see so many of them in Sunderland. It still blows my mind when I look into the crowd at England matches and see all the cowboy hats, because it really was something that started out as just a bit of fun.

While it was great for me to get the celebration out at the Stadium of Light, my favourite moment of that game was the try I created for Jess. We attacked from deep inside our 22, moving the ball into space after a USA turnover, and we backed ourselves to do it. Everything happened so quickly.

When I picked up possession, the try-line seemed a long way away. I wouldn't go so far as to say that what I did next is something you can't coach, but at the same time it's not something I would ever practise in the build-up to a game either. It summed up the belief Mitch had given me – to do what I thought was right and back my own ability to the hilt. I think it's fair to say my childhood playing football also came through at that moment.

As I ran down the touchline, I put boot to ball. You never know how a rugby ball is going to bounce and that's the beauty of it. But as I chased forward, it sat up beautifully for me on the halfway line. I controlled it briefly on my thigh, the ball popping up into my arms. I then swerved my hips to avoid the cover tackle and ran into space before drawing the last defender and passing to Jess to score. The try soon blew up on TikTok and Instagram. It was all over my phone when I looked at it after the game. That try is one I watch back now and smile at. Could I have caught the ball instead of using my thigh? Probably. But that wasn't what my mind was telling me to do at that point. My instinct, despite the pressure of it being a World Cup opener, told me to go with the thigh and that's what I did. Two tries, an assist, a big win and a player-of-the-match award was a great way to start the World Cup. But now it was underway, we just wanted more. We couldn't wait to get out there and play again.

From Sunderland, we travelled south to the Midlands to play Samoa in Northampton, and then Australia in Brighton.

CHAPTER 12

As we moved around the country, you could feel the energy building. Sunderland had been fantastic, but day by day, game by game, I got a sense of something special brewing. I loved the fact we didn't just stay in one place. Sunderland was just the start. In our downtime, we'd go out for coffee and I found that as the tournament progressed, more and more people would start to recognise me.

I was on the bench for the 92-3 hammering of Samoa in which Jess scored a hat-trick. Again, me being rested had been part of Mitch's plan all along. At the final whistle, we came together with the amateur Samoan players for a giant huddle. We sang and danced, both teams celebrating the joy that came with playing at a World Cup. It was a special moment. Afterwards, Chloe Kelly came into our changing rooms. I'd met quite a few of the Lionesses previously at different events, but for Chloe to come to one of our games in person was huge. Her profile had gone to another level after her winning penalty against Spain. Chloe being in the changing room and posing for pictures with the players reminded us again of why we were playing this World Cup. It wasn't just for ourselves. There was the bigger picture of growing women's rugby. It was very special to know that people we looked up to, like Chloe, had been inspired by what we were doing and were showing that love back. We definitely felt that support. It's not something we need to ask for now. It just happens.

Australia in Brighton was our final pool game and the first real test of our World Cup credentials. Although the final result was a convincing 47-7 victory, the game didn't go to plan. It certainly didn't for me, anyway. We knew the Wallaroos were a very dangerous team and would be a step up on the USA and Samoa. That was demonstrated in the first half. We only led 19-7 at the break and, to be honest, I felt like I'd let everyone down. I had a poor first 40 minutes. As a full-back, one of your main jobs is covering the back field and cutting out opposition kicks. Australia badly exposed us with their kicking game, and a lot of that was down to my own poor performance. Although we were ahead, I wasn't feeling too great about myself. The team talked about making changes to counteract Australia's excellent kicking, and I was excited to get back out there for the second period. I was desperate to make amends.

You can have all the best intentions in the world, but sometimes things get taken out of your hands. In the 46th minute, I carried the ball forwards and got hit by a double Australian tackle. I fell forwards. My head hit the ground, bouncing off the Amex Stadium turf with a horrible whack. It was an awful knock. I was very briefly knocked out, the force of my head's collision with the ground rendering me unconscious. I hadn't realised it had happened at first. But when I tried to sit up, I realised quickly I wasn't right. I was very, very groggy.

Thankfully, I hadn't experienced a concussion before that point, although a World Cup was a bad moment for it to happen for the first time. As rugby players in 2026, we are very aware of the dangers of head injuries. The treatment we get from our physios is first class. Player welfare is hugely important and I think rugby has made great strides in this area. For example, with England we wear instrumented mouthguards with sensors

CHAPTER 12

in them that measure the size of impacts and collisions. If they exceed a key marker point, you have to come off for a head injury assessment (HIA). That wasn't needed in my case against Australia, as I was experiencing and showing several clear signs of concussion. The fact I'd been knocked out meant I was never, ever going to be going back on the field. When I came round, I'm not afraid to admit I was really scared. I was confused as to what had happened and felt incredibly dazed. With the help of medics, I managed to slowly get to my feet before being led away down the tunnel where I was analysed and well looked after.

There was no cognitive testing to be done at that point, because I did not need an HIA. The priority was my well-being. I'd been able to walk off the field after the head injury, though of course at the time I wasn't sure what was going to happen next. After I'd been treated and felt well enough to do so, I made my way back out to the bench for the rest of the second half. I wanted to show the fans I was okay. I was delighted that when I appeared on the big screen and waved to the crowd, I received a huge cheer from the England supporters. That meant a massive amount to me. Thankfully, the team pulled away in the second half to record a comfortable win.

The Princess of Wales was the headline attraction at the Australia game. She watched it from the Brighton stands with Zoe, who was out with a short-term knee injury. I might have been far from 100 per cent, but when the Princess came down to the changing room afterwards, I asked her if she would put a cowboy hat on. To be honest, I've got no idea how you're supposed to behave around the royal family. But, as I saw it, if the Princess was with us in the changing rooms, and we had cowboy hats there, then she had to become a cowboy! The Princess's answer was a strong 'yes'. She was so lovely – very well-spoken, as you can imagine. My overriding memory of our meeting was just how elegant she was. It was a privilege to be in the same room as her, let alone talk to her. We discussed the World Cup and the growth of women's sport and had a picture together. It was so good of her to show us her support. We didn't get her to do the cowboy dance, mainly because I didn't feel up to it. The picture is on my parents' mantlepiece at home in Riddlesden. It's one I'll always savour – a special memory from what was, on a personal level, a deeply frustrating and worrying day.

13
Dreamland

I knew as soon as I'd been injured in the game against Australia that I would miss the quarter-final. The mandatory 12-day stand-down period after a concussion meant that for my World Cup dream to stay alive, I needed the team to beat Scotland without me. It was a brutal blow. I'd waited three years for this tournament and, all of a sudden, there was a chance I could have played my last game in it. If we lost to Scotland, our World Cup would end there and then. And what happened in that game was absolutely out of my control.

Concussion affects everyone differently. Having not suffered a concussion previously, I knew I had to be very careful and I did very little in the days that followed the match in Brighton. I just got on with it. It was the same as the hamstring injury in the Six Nations. Sometimes, you have to accept the cards you've been dealt.

In the days that followed, I didn't really have splitting headaches. It was similar to jetlag. I just felt incredibly tired. It was my body's way of telling me that my brain had been injured and that the only way for it to recover was to rest. So, that's exactly what I did.

CHAPTER 13

I did a lot of sleeping. Fretting about the Scotland game was not going to help my head heal, so I had to try and relax. Helena Rowland, who had performed so impressively when she replaced me against Australia, continued at full-back against Scotland. I needn't have worried. Helena was brilliant once again, and Zoe was back from her knee injury to play her first game since the USA. By that point, Bristol had become our home for the knock-out rounds before the final, and Ashton Gate was a sea of white and red for a 40-8 victory over Scotland. I spent a lot of that game watching from the stands, banging away on a drum to show my support for the girls.

When you suffer a concussion, you have to complete return-to-play protocols. Essentially, what that means is you must complete and pass all sorts of cognitive tests, to show your brain has recovered, before you can train or play again. Being forced to do nothing for 12 days post-Australia certainly helped, although I knew it meant I would be light on training minutes ahead of our semi-final with old rivals France. At the same time, I was aware that Helena had played very, very well while I was on the sidelines. I couldn't be sure I'd be back in the team for the last four.

Thankfully, by 18 September – 12 days after the Australia game and just two before we were due to face France – I'd ticked all the right boxes and passed the return-to-play protocols. Even though a World Cup semi-final was on the horizon, I took absolutely no risks with my welfare. When I was told I'd be able to face France, and that Mitch had selected me for the team, I must admit that my overriding feeling was one of relief. My

World Cup was back on track. I felt absolutely fine for France and was delighted that Mitch showed faith in me by putting me straight back into the starting line-up.

We knew what to expect from France. We'd played them so many times during the build-up to the World Cup, almost always in Grand Slam deciders. And although we were no strangers to big games, a World Cup semi-final was certainly on another level. As a team, we'd laid down a big marker to Les Bleues with our decisive victory over them in the tournament warm-up on French soil. That gave us confidence and a sense that we had momentum behind us. We also had home advantage. Although my training time had been limited, we'd had a great week of preparation. The fact both our quarter-final and semi-final were in Bristol was another thing in our favour. As good as it was to have done plenty of travelling in the pool stages, come the World Cup's business end it helped to have a settled base.

But we also knew France had only come up one point short in our Six Nations game earlier that year. It meant there was absolutely no complacency in our ranks, even though France had players absent due to injury and suspension.

I felt ready. I felt fit. And within the first five minutes, I was given the chance to show it. I'd already had an early run with the ball, which gave me confidence. Then, from a scrappy ruck in midfield, Amy Cokayne picked up the ball. I was on the left wing, with forwards Hannah Botterman and Abbie Ward inside me. Hannah had also missed the Scotland game, after suffering a back injury against Australia. Like me, she was hungry to get back into World Cup action. We soon combined. The forwards'

CHAPTER 13

handling, which put me into space, was brilliant play. Hannah drew in two French defenders before offloading to me, giving me space down the touchline on halfway. I put on the afterburners – just as I had done when playing cops and robbers at home in Riddlesden all those years ago – and cut inside the last covering French defender, Kelly Arbey, to score next to the posts. In just a matter of seconds, that try totally took away all the frustration I'd felt from missing the Scotland game. As good as that feeling was, I couldn't allow myself to get carried away – we were in a very tight match. After my early try, we made far more errors than we'd have liked, and France were very much in the contest at half time. We had just a two-point lead. Our mistakes were keeping France within touching distance. But the mood was very calm during the break. There was no shouting and swearing.

A rolling maul try from Amy was a great start to the second half, and we moved to 21-12 ahead when Abbie crashed over. It gave us some breathing room. In the 68th minute, we had a scrum on our own 10-metre line. What followed next might have looked a bit bizarre to those watching in the stands at Ashton Gate, or at home on BBC, but I can tell you: it was absolutely planned. From the set-piece, Lucy Packer passed the ball to Zoe Harrison, our fly-half. When we'd discussed what the move should be, Zoe had said to me: 'I'm just going to kick the ball straight at her and as hard as I can.' Zoe was referring to Marine Ménager, the French wing and captain. I'd had a bit of a scuffle with Ménager in the first half. It was nothing nasty or untoward, but it ended with me putting my finger to my lips to tell her to be quiet. That's me to a tee – a bit cheeky and combative, but not someone who oversteps the mark. Things haven't changed since school! Regardless of that, I trusted Zoe Harrison's plans implicitly. Whether it's her or Holly Aitchison at fly-half, the No. 10 calls the shots. As it turned out, it was a pretty good call.

Zoe smashed the ball with brute force at Ménager, even though she was more than 20 metres or so away. The pre-planned aim was to force the French player into a mistake. Ménager attempted to control it with her foot. Given the speed at which the ball was travelling it was a risky move and, perhaps unsurprisingly, her touch was heavy as a result. I was chasing Zoe's kick, thinking I would be forced into a tackle, but knowing that if there was any mistake I would be there to capitalise. That's exactly what happened. The ball rebounded off Ménager's foot and straight to me. The bounce couldn't have been more perfect, allowing me to collect possession on the run without breaking my stride. It meant I had momentum as soon as the ball was in my hands. That's key to speed, and my pace took me past three French defenders and all the way to the line. It was a crucial score, because it was the one that put the game to bed and sealed our place in the final.

The noise as I ran to the line was deafening, but I had to remain cool until I put the ball down. When I did, there was just an outpouring of emotion. After the worries over the hamstring injury at the start of the year and the concussion against Australia, this was a moment to celebrate. I'd done a lot of hard work to get to that point, coming through some tough times. But the adversity you have to deal with in professional

CHAPTER 13

rugby is all worth it for the good days, like reaching a World Cup final. At the full-time whistle, while knowing there was still one more hurdle to overcome, I felt a sense of accomplishment. I'd scored two tries to keep my team on track for the goal we'd been working towards for three years. I was named player of the match, and I'll never forget the cheer my name got when that was announced over the Ashton Gate Tannoy.

While I was pleased with my performance and considered it my best of the World Cup so far, I felt that I'd somewhat stolen the award from others. I thought our forwards were absolutely incredible against France. Hannah produced a monumental performance, stealing the ball with crucial turnovers at key moments. Any one of those forwards could have been the star performer.

Reaching the final was all we'd been dreaming of. But achieving that would mean nothing if we didn't deliver in the biggest game of all. A World Cup final at Allianz Stadium in front of a sold-out crowd of more than 80,000 had always been the target. Now there was only one team standing between us and the trophy. Except it was a different team from the one most of us had expected to be facing.

Everyone thought an England–New Zealand final, a repeat of the 2022 decider, was the most likely outcome. The Black Ferns had beaten England in the World Cup finals in both 2017 and 2022 and were rightly considered one of the game's best sides. The trophy was theirs to defend and they were doing a good job of it. That was until they ran into Canada in their semi-final – which took place the night before our last-four tie with France. We knew how good a side Canada were, but their performance in Bristol to beat New Zealand 34-19 was outstanding. The Canadians played some brilliant attacking rugby. They played at a pace the Black Ferns couldn't keep up with, which is saying something. We were well aware not only of how good Canada were as a team, but also of the incredible story of how they got to the tournament. Despite being real World Cup contenders, and going into the tournament as No. 2 in the World Rugby rankings, the Canadian outfit wasn't fully professional. In order to try and win in England, Rugby Canada had launched a $1 million fundraising campaign to support their players with additional training camps. We were aware of it because of all the coverage it got in the media. However, whether they were amateur or professional made no difference. Canada had phenomenal players. Their captain Sophie de Goede and wing Asia Hogan-Rochester had both been in exceptional form, so we knew the size of the task ahead.

We couldn't focus too much on Canada, however. Ultimately, we were in a World Cup final and our mantra as an England team has always been to focus on ourselves. Even though we were preparing for the biggest game of our lives, we stuck to that process. Mitch had been big on continuity in selection since taking charge. Yes, at times he'd rotated the team during the World Cup. But there was a familiarity to the side that was a big help to us starting players. There was a calmness to the team throughout that week. Training was to a high standard. Everything was on point, but there was still time for fun, with Meg Jones cycling to training and giving Mo a lift on her bike.

CHAPTER 13

We all knew the pressure was on us to win the World Cup. But we hadn't been inhibited by that throughout the tournament and that wasn't going to change in the week of the final.

To mark such an important match, I had something special planned: I was going to wear a pair of new, custom-made boots. Since March 2021, I'd been working closely with Canterbury, who are an established rugby kit brand. I have a great relationship with their senior vice president Simon Rowe. From our first meeting, we had discussed my interest in fashion and art and creating women-specific rugby products. As such, my role was part ambassador and part consultant.

Before the World Cup started, Canterbury approached me with the idea of me designing my own boots. They told me that it would be the first time rugby boots had been designed by a player from the women's game. I thought that was pretty cool. I'd always worn either white or bright colours. I've got this thing that I hate wearing dark boots because, in my head, it makes my feet feel heavy. There's probably no scientific truth to that, but that's how I feel and it's the reason why I've always had white boots with Canterbury. They just make my feet feel light, which means I can dance around the pitch the way I need to. Canterbury asked me to come up with a few designs, so, before the World Cup, I downloaded a number of design applications onto my iPad and got to work.

My overriding thought was: 'How can I make myself feel even faster and lighter on the field?' That's where the idea of the cheetah came in. Obviously, the cheetah is a very, very fast, predator. And I also knew that cheetah and leopard print were fashionable at the time. I put the words 'show' on the back of the left boot, and 'time' on the back of the right, with a little smiley face making the 'o' of 'show'. There were two reasons for that. I try to see a game of rugby as like a show. Players train so hard to put in big performances and be successful as individuals and as a team. But I think it's really important to understand we are on the field to entertain, too. If people come and pay their hard-earned money to watch a match, they want to see something special from the stands. That's what I try to provide. By seeing rugby as a show, it really helps me take the pressure off myself. The World Cup final was no different.

Before every match, I also put tape on each of my wrists. I pen a few symbols on them. A butterfly is one and a sunflower is another. The butterfly is for someone who passed away who was very close to me. They had butterflies all over their house, and drawing one on my wrist is a reminder that person is always with me during matches.

For me, a sunflower radiates energy. I want to be someone that radiates energy on the pitch. I also draw a smiley face on my tape. That tells me that when our backs are against the wall, or when there are moments when I'm feeling quite isolated in a game, I must still smile because, ultimately, I'm incredibly fortunate to enjoy what I do. That was as true for a World Cup final as it was for any previous match.

The 27th of September 2025. A day I'll never, ever forget. By the time the morning of the final arrived, there was a real but quiet confidence in the team, though that never, ever edged into arrogance or carelessness. We all had a sense of: 'This is it

CHAPTER 13

now.' Whatever was going to happen was going to happen. We'd done all the hard work, on and off the field, and by the Saturday morning, all we needed to do was get to the game, allow it to play out, and have trust in our ability, processes and plan. That's exactly what we did. There was nothing different about it. Given the magnitude of the match, people might expect our preparation to have been altered. But I can honestly say that we did nothing different.

On the morning of the game, I received a text from my mum. It read:

> Remember that feeling after you'd lost the World Cup final. You just wanted to play it all over again. Today you can and you will win. X

I was determined to not be left feeling as I had after the 2022 final. And, in my head, that was never going to happen, because it was a new tournament and this time we had the support of a home crowd.

For the 2025 final, we had home surroundings at The Lensbury Hotel in Teddington, which is just a short drive to Allianz Stadium. The hours before the game were all about keeping cool and collected. As I've already mentioned, on the morning of any match, the biggest thing for me is to sort my hair out. For the semi-final with France, I'd put my hair in braids because it was forecast to rain and I didn't want a repeat of the Scotland 2024 wet dog look! I didn't want it to go in my eyes or become a distraction. But for the final, I had all of my curls on show. Doing my hair is a nice way of preparing for a match. I normally do my hair before the second team meeting starts. I have the same processes. There's nothing really normal about getting ready to play in a World Cup final, but you have to try your best to treat it like any other game. I reminded myself throughout the week to stay in the moment, enjoy the company of the people I was with and – most importantly of all – to make sure my hair looked nice!

'YAWA' by Fireboy DML had been my personal song of the World Cup. It's a classic Afrobeat song, the sort I love. We'd all dance and sing to it before matches, filmed by Maddie Feaunati, who'd then post the video to Instagram or TikTok. The music really helped us get in the mood. My pre-match meal was the same as always – just a bowl of plain pasta. There are no frills to it and it's pretty boring, but at that point I just see food as fuel. It's what I need for the game and nothing more than that.

The RFU had been clear two years before the tournament that its aim was to sell out Allianz Stadium for the final. At the time, that seemed to many like an ambitious target. But it is also exactly what happened. Over the past few years we had become used to playing in front of huge crowds, and we'd played at Allianz Stadium several times. So, while this was a World Cup final, it wasn't totally uncharted territory for us. But, at the same time, we also knew an 82,000 sell-out would be the biggest attendance for any women's rugby match ever, and that we were going to be making history.

When we arrived at the ground and our team bus pulled in to the west car park, we were blown away by what we saw. It

CHAPTER 13

was one thing knowing the number of spectators who would be there. But it was quite another to actually see what we witnessed as we got off the bus and walked into the stadium. The place was packed. At ground level, there were cowboy hats and England flags everywhere. There were drums beating and fireworks going off. But what you saw when you looked up above took my breath away. It felt like fans were hanging off every corner of the west and south stands to get a glimpse of us. During the build-up to the World Cup, and then into the tournament itself, our support had grown steadily. But this was another level. While I like to listen to my Afrobeats music on the way to matches, so had my earphones in, it was also vitally important I took in all that was happening around me. It was a defining game for women's rugby in England and had an atmosphere to match. We didn't lack motivation, but the scenes on our arrival only served to reinforce to us how big the match was. We weren't just playing for ourselves. If we could win the final, it would be about much more than success for us as a team. In 80 minutes, we had the capacity to change women's rugby in England for ever. It was a challenge I couldn't wait to get stuck into.

You know when something happens to you in slow motion? It's happened to me a few times in my life so far and I'm sure it's an experience many other people have had. That's how I would describe my World Cup final try. Nobody panicked when Hogan-Rochester opened the scoring for Canada with a try in the corner that put us 5-0 behind. Everyone just kept doing their jobs, confident that if we did we'd score sooner rather than later.

We just needed to stay very calm. This game was the 'jungle' Mitch had been referring to, and we were ready to perform in it. In the seventh minute, a high tackle – illegal under rugby's rules – by De Goede meant we had a penalty advantage. When Mo passed me the ball, I knew I had nothing to lose. I wouldn't be the player I am without the team I have around me. But at the same time, I've always tried to be someone who comes up with big moments in big games. Then my body just took over. What happened next wasn't thought-driven. It was entirely natural, based purely on instinct.

I shifted my feet very quickly to beat the first Canadian defender and saw space open up in front of me. From there, I knew I could make it to the line, even though there was still a lot of work to do. It was during that run to the line that everything slowed down. There were just nine seconds between me catching the ball and putting it down between the posts. But it felt like a lifetime. It was a really odd feeling. As I got to the line, I thought to myself: 'S*** I'd better score now after all that!' It was fight or flight and I chose flight! The slow-motion feeling only ended when Jess jumped on me to celebrate, knocking me out of the stupor I'd fallen into. It was very surreal, almost like an out-of-body experience. Only it was all very real. My ears popped because the noise from the celebrating crowd was so loud.

I am a full-back and finisher; that's my job. In the same way your props are expected to scrum, your back three is expected to score. I was just proud to put the team on the board, but I have to say scoring in front of 81,885 in a home World Cup final and a record BBC television audience of 5.8 million was a feeling

CHAPTER 13

that will be hard to beat. Everyone who was at Allianz Stadium that day knew they were going to be part of history, and also part of shaping the future. As I ran back for the restart, I was still in a bit of shock at what had happened. The try was similar to the ones I'd scored in the semi-final against France. It reconfirmed to me that winning the World Cup was just meant to be, even if at that point there was still a long way to go in the game.

As a full-back, you get the chance to score tries and come up with moments of magic. But that's not possible without the forwards delivering. In the World Cup final, that's exactly what happened. My try got us back in the game, but the pack laid the platform for the dominant performance that followed. It was fitting that the other try scorers were Amy Cokayne, Abbie Ward and Alex Matthews, who crossed twice. It didn't matter to me if I scored again or not; the only thing anyone cared about was the win. Just because you haven't crossed that try line, it doesn't mean you've had a bad performance. Hannah Botterman was yellow-carded in the second half and Hogan-Rochester capitalised on Canada's superior numbers to score her second, but we were 20 points clear as the clock ticked into the red zone. When the referee Hollie Davidson decided our last rolling maul had been held up and blew the final whistle, Allianz Stadium erupted. After all we'd gone through, and the disappointment of the last World Cup final, the overriding feeling was one of pure delight. It was a complete contrast in emotions to when Davidson had called an end to the 2022 match at Eden Park. On that occasion, the overriding feeling had been despair. This time, it was elation. And relief. We'd achieved what we'd set out to do.

The 33-13 win was our 33rd successive victory, but by far our most important, as it cemented our status as champions of the world. I hugged Meg and Helena first. I was as delighted for Meg as much as myself, given everything she'd been through. As the fireworks and plumes of smoke went off and Zoe Stratford lifted the trophy, we jumped into each other's arms and got the party started. I was thinking to myself: 'There is no other team I would rather be in than this one.' The England squad that lifted the 2025 World Cup had a connection and a bond within it that I'd not felt before. I'd long believed that sense of togetherness would be one of the reasons we could win a World Cup. And that is exactly what happened, our victory providing the icing on the cake of a glorious summer for women's sport in England. We'd followed in the footsteps of the Lionesses by not only having success as a team but by changing how women's sport in our country is seen. It is now more popular than ever and part of the fabric of our society. In the end, I was right. Winning the World Cup had been written for us. I've long felt you might not ever know why things work out the way they do for you. Everyone experiences highs and lows, and I'm no different.

But as I stood on the Allianz Stadium pitch, with the World Cup in my hands and a cowboy hat on my head, all the pain of the toughest moments I'd endured had completely melted away. We'd done it.

14

Sports Personality and MBE

The weeks and months that followed the World Cup final win over Canada were a blur. In November, I received a double whammy of news, each part of a magnitude that I struggled to comprehend.

The first came when I was on a train back to Reading from London after a sponsorship appearance. I had a text from my agent, Ben: 'Congratulations. Mad about Sports Personality of the Year, isn't it?' I had no idea what he was talking about. I was so confused. I called him back straight away. He told me I'd been nominated for the prestigious BBC gong. The BBC Sports Personality of the Year award is handed out on an annual basis to a sportsman or woman who is deemed to have stood out for their achievements in that calendar year. I was on a six-person shortlist alongside golfing superstar Rory McIlroy, McClaren driver Lando Norris – who had just been crowned Formula 1 world champion – and darts No. 1 Luke Littler. Lionesses Hannah Hampton and Chloe Kelly were also nominated, meaning three of the six were female athletes. That was a reflection of what a brilliant year 2025 had been for women's sport in England. Finding out about my nomination was an incredible moment,

CHAPTER 14

but I was by myself on the train, and it felt odd having no one to share it with. I asked Ben if I could tell my mum and dad the news. He said I could, but that no one else could know because the shortlist was not yet public knowledge. So, there I was on a busy train to Reading, on the phone to my mum and dad, trying to whisper to them that I'd been nominated for Sports Personality of the Year. I had to keep really quiet so that the other passengers couldn't overhear what I was saying.

At the end of November, I flew to Dubai for the Dubai Sevens. I, of course, love rugby's shorter format, and I was really looking forward to attending. Only this time, I wasn't playing. Instead, I was travelling as an ambassador for the bank HSBC, who are one of the tournament's biggest sponsors. I was in a taxi with rugby legends Jason Robinson, Bryan Habana and Ruby Tui when my phone pinged with a message from my England teammate Sadia Kabeya. Her message just said: 'Have you received an email?'

I was intrigued and went to check my inbox. The number of unread emails had, at that point, grown to 32,000, so I had a lot to look through. Then I spotted an email from an account I didn't recognise. The subject was: 'NY 2026 Honours List'. Maybe this was what Sadia was messaging about? Or maybe it was spam? I hovered over it, then opened it up, hoping that it wasn't someone who was going to steal all my personal data. When I read the contents, I was blown away to see the news I was to be named a Member of the Order of the British Empire (MBE) – a prestigious award in the UK honours system that recognises outstanding achievement or service to the community with a significant, long-term impact. I was stunned. The email was marked 'strictly confidential', because, again, the news wasn't going to be made public for a number of weeks. So, sitting there in the taxi with Robinson, Habana and Tui, I had to keep it totally to myself. It was pretty hard to keep a straight face. But was it actually real?

It was only a few hours later, when we were at a sponsorship dinner near the Burj Khalifa, Dubai's iconic skyscraper, that I found two minutes to escape to the privacy of the toilet, where I could read the email in full. It was then that I realised it was definitely genuine. I was to be awarded an MBE for my role in England's World Cup victory. I just felt an overriding sense of shock. I knew these sorts of honours were given to people who have done amazing things, but I wasn't sure I deserved to be in such a category.

Our coach John Mitchell, captain Zoe Stratford and flanker Marlie Packer were to be made Officers of the Order of the British Empire (OBE). Like me, Sadia and Megan Jones were also to become MBEs. The news was to be officially confirmed at the end of December in the King's New Year Honours List. I was hugely proud of the other girls who had been recognised for their achievements. But I think there's so many more of the girls that should have been given an honour as well. No individual can play well without the whole team, so, if anything, the whole squad should have been acknowledged, because rugby is a team sport.

Being nominated for Sports Personality and becoming an MBE were things I could only have dreamed of. Both were huge for me. I soon learned I was the first female rugby player to

CHAPTER 14

ever make the Sports Personality shortlist, and the first English rugby player – male or female – to be up for the award since Jonny Wilkinson and Jason Robinson in 2007. I wasn't worried about whether I'd win or not. For me, being nominated was big enough. Any of us could have been nominated for the individual award. Luckily, it wasn't just about me: the England women's rugby side been nominated for the Sports Personality team of the year award, alongside the Lionesses and Team Europe, who had just won golf's Ryder Cup by beating the USA. That sort of recognition – be it individual or collective – only helps to put women's rugby on an even greater platform. Women's rugby players have been told for years that no one was bothered about coming to watch us play. I am so proud that we turned things around by winning a World Cup, inspiring a nation, and receiving two nominations for Sports Personality. I want more and more people to be aware of it.

Other than my mum and dad, I didn't mention the Sports Personality award shortlisting to anyone. But then, the night before the nomination got released, our media team sent a message to the England player WhatsApp group chat to let everyone know. What I found so special were the messages I got from my teammates. They see me all the time, so they didn't have to say anything. I think all the girls saw the good my nomination could do for women's rugby as a whole, putting it on a pedestal for the first time. It was really heartwarming to feel the love. The fact that they all dropped me a little message or put supportive posts on their social media accounts made me feel very warm inside.

SPORTS PERSONALITY AND MBE

Growing up, I would always prefer to be outside playing cops and robbers and other games to sitting on the sofa watching television. But I'd always known how big Sports Personality of the Year was. In both 2023 and 2024, I'd been fortunate enough to attend the event.

When you're in the room surrounded by all these amazing athletes from all different sports, it doesn't matter what you look like or where you're from. I'm a strong believer that we're all people before we are athletes. More than that, everyone deserves to be there, because everyone's got that common ground of having the mindset needed to be at the top of their sport. I loved that. I remember seeing the Lionesses at the 2023 Awards, and just being hugely inspired by the fact I was in the same room as them.

At the 2024 awards, I remember watching the athlete Keely Hodgkinson win and telling myself that I would be nominated the following year. Sometimes dreams do come true. I'd had a sense, going into the World Cup year of 2025, that something big was coming, even though I wasn't sure what it was. But I remembered what Oliver Wilson had told me all those years ago at school in East Morton: 'Ellie, I think you're going to be famous when you're older.' Now, while I certainly wasn't an A-list celebrity by any stretch, Oliver's words were starting to feel prophetic.

I drove up from Reading to Manchester on the morning of 18 December for the Sports Personality awards feeling nervous, but excited. Having been before, I knew what the evening involved, but being nominated for the first time added a whole new dimension.

CHAPTER 14

As usual for me, the night before was chaotic.

I did a little bit of packing at around 11pm. All the girls at both Harlequins and England had been asking me for weeks what I was going to wear for the ceremony. On the morning of the event, I still didn't know what dress I was going for. Classic me. I asked the stylist who was helping me to bring two options that were completely different. All the girls were asking: 'Does that not stress you out?' It didn't at all because I'd tried on both options in advance and they looked nice. In the past, I've gone to other events in dresses I'd never even tried on, so to me, I felt well prepared!

The memory I'll cherish the most from the 2025 Sports Personality awards is that, because our England side was nominated for the team award, all my teammates attended too. When I arrived in Manchester, I had my hair and makeup done and I settled on a dress with the stylist. I went for a white number with a big slit down the leg. The rest of the girls, who were in a different hotel, got ready together, and our WhatsApp group chat was pinging with messages of excitement. My mum and dad and my brother Sam and his girlfriend had come along with me, so I wasn't on my own. One thing that's really important to me is that I share experiences with those closest to me. I've been fortunate to do some really cool things on the back of playing rugby, but they mean more to me if I do them alongside my loved ones.

My mum had her hair and makeup done too. I got to the event before my teammates and had to walk down a red carpet, pose for pictures, and do lots of media interviews. Then I was shown into a separate room where I was told all the details for the evening, like where I was going to be sat, when I was going to go on stage and how the awards would be handed out. I didn't actually realise until then that I was due to go on stage. Walking in heels and a dress with a long trail is not as simple as you might think, so I started practising straight away.

It was then that I was given a media briefing sheet, designed to make sure I stayed on message during my on-stage interview. I never read a media brief. Lewis Hancock, our media officer with England, will confirm this is true. If I'm going to do an interview, I'd rather give authentic answers and speak from the heart than regurgitate what I'm supposed to say after learning lines from a sheet. Whenever I read or watch an interview, I can tell straight away if someone's speaking from a script. I much prefer hearing something you don't expect from an athlete. As the profile of women's rugby has grown, we've done so much media training to avoid getting in trouble that I think there's a danger we'll all end up sounding the same. I don't want to be like that.

I've done a lot of media interviews now, so I feel comfortable in that environment. I know how to answer questions, even if they're difficult. There have been some in the past that have thrown me, but you only learn from experience. Now, I actually like it if I get asked outside-of-the-box questions. I often say that if I'm only going to be asked about my rugby career, the journalist could do the piece on me just by looking me up on Wikipedia. I've always liked to speak my mind without worrying what others might think, and Sports Personality wasn't going to be any different. I was more anxious about the fact that one of

CHAPTER 14

the straps on my heels had broken than any possible question I might get asked. The other concern was that my dress, with its high slit, was the sort that you can't wear underwear with. My mum kept mouthing at me: 'Be careful of your dress!' At one point before the ceremony I was sat down and went to uncross and cross my legs – I almost flashed the whole world. My mum nearly got on her hands and knees and crawled over to tell me to stop moving my legs about. My modesty was preserved and, although my heel wouldn't stay on, we found some emergency tape and I went down to see the rest of the England girls when they arrived.

As usual, it was an amazing evening, full of moving sporting stories. When I was asked to go up on stage to speak about winning the World Cup and my journey to this point, I wanted to stay and watch the video about me. I'd done a big interview for it a few weeks before but hadn't seen the end product. Thankfully, there was a small screen backstage playing it live, so I watched it as I waited to go on. It really touched me. My teammates Jess Breach and Megan Jones and all my old coaches and teachers were so kind about me. It made me realise just what I'd been through to become a World Cup winner.

When I walked out on stage to speak to Gabby Logan, who was one of the presenters, all I could do was smile and giggle. That's because all my England teammates were cheering for me like mad. Then I saw my mum, dad and brother going bonkers too. They were such a reassuring presence.

But I was really nervous – unusually so for me – when I sat down on the sofa to talk. Not because of what I might be asked, but because this moment was far bigger and more important than just me. I realised that while women's rugby is much more visible now – and that's huge in itself – the players of today need to keep driving that forward. That's why I felt a bit of pressure. I saw it as me speaking on behalf of women's rugby. As I did my speech, my legs were shaking.

After I'd spoken and sat back down in my seat, Clare Balding – who was one of the other presenters – looked over at me while she was preparing for her next segment. She mouthed at me: 'That interview was amazing.' Clare also put her thumbs up. That really calmed me down. Then, later, when I was back in my seat, all of a sudden it was announced the phone lines had closed. The Sports Personality shortlist is drawn up by a panel of experts, but the voting for the winner is open to the public. It had been explained to us that the three athletes who had received the most votes would be announced in alphabetical order (using the athlete's first name), before then being ranked.

The nerves returned. I was not expecting to be in the top three, but nevertheless I wasn't sure how I was going to react when the names were read out, and I knew the television camera would be on me. I quickly worked out that if the presenters said Hannah Hampton's name before mine, I wouldn't be in the top three. But I was called out first, which meant I'd at the very least finished third.

I couldn't believe it. The nerves disappeared again. I was in a world of my own when football legend Thierry Henry came on stage to announce who had won. When he read out my name as runner-up, with Lando Norris in third, I totally glazed over.

CHAPTER 14

In my head, I was just getting ready to clap Rory McIlroy as the winner. That's why I ended up looking as if I was stuck in my seat and my dad, who was behind me, had to shake me out of my stupor to tell me I had to go back up on stage. McIlroy's amazing achievements in winning the Masters to complete a clean sweep of golf's majors, and also helping Team Europe to win the Ryder Cup, meant he was a more-than-deserving winner. For me to even be mentioned in the same sporting conversation as someone like him was just incredible. As McIlroy was presented with the winner's award, while music played and the fireworks went off, I was stood with my runner-up trophy next to Henry. I tried to take everything in around me, but it was all barely believable.

It was a shame that the Red Roses didn't win the team of the year award – Europe's Ryder Cup side took that gong to complete a golfing double. I was a bit disappointed by that, but as the end credits rolled, it dawned on me that by finishing second in Sports Personality, I'd achieved something massive individually, and also helped the sport I love in the same breath.

I felt like a winner after the show ended, especially when we went to the afterparty. It was the first time I'd seen the rest of the England girls, and we all had a picture together, with me holding my trophy. The girls made me feel so celebrated and so special, putting me on their shoulders and dancing up and down. I've had lots of individual accolades, like being Six Nations player of the Championship, World Rugby player of the year and now Sports Personality runner-up and MBE. But I'm also aware I'm just an outside back who wouldn't have done anything at all without the rest of the team I play in. That is why celebrating at Sports Personality alongside those with whom I'd won the World Cup meant that an individual award felt like a collective success. That's how it seemed to me, anyway. I hope my teammates felt the same.

At the afterparty, we all gathered together in a big circle to sing, dance and celebrate. We sang 'Jar of Hearts' again – the tune that had become our unofficial World Cup anthem. I think our group must have had good energy because others soon got involved. Angry Ginge, the YouTuber and winner of *I'm a Celebrity... Get Me Out of Here!* was on the microphone and leading the charge.

It was an incredible evening, but as the excitement died down the following day and I headed home, I started to feel anxious. In just two days' time I was due to play for Harlequins against Bristol Bears at Allianz Stadium in the club's traditional 'Big Game' double header. Harlequins' men's and women's teams play their home matches at Twickenham Stoop, just across the road from Allianz Stadium. But each Christmas, we play one game at the home of English rugby. It's a phenomenal occasion and a great chance to play a club match in front of a huge crowd.

I was very aware that 'Big Game' means more eyes are on the match than normal, and that would only be amplified by me finishing second at Sports Personality. I knew people would be watching me, some for the first time. I called my mum on the drive back down south. 'Mum, I feel a bit of pressure here. People saw me at Sports Personality and two days later I've got a game.' I felt I had a big point to prove, and maybe that feeling was intensified by some of the social media comments I'd seen after the awards. I like to use social media, but of course it comes with a downside. There will always be those who want to criticise.

It might be better not to read the comments and give any credence to the trolls. But the truth is I do read everything on my posts, particularly on Instagram. I know there'll be things I don't like. I've had to warn my mum and dad about what they might read about me online. I'd say at least 80 per cent of the stuff about me is positive, but there are also trolls who post things those closest to me might not want to see. There are some people who still hate on women's rugby. 'Who even is she?' became a familiar comment in my feed after Sports Personality. There are others who might try and sexualise me. That happened when I posted a picture of myself in a bikini in Dubai after the World Cup.

Even though I read all the comments I get – good and bad – I ignore the haters. I don't reply, I just love proving people wrong and try to do that through deeds not words. The trolls fuel me and only add to my motivation. Going into the Bristol game, I was determined to show the 'Who even is she?' brigade what I could do. I wanted people who might have been watching me for the first time to say: 'Oh that's Ellie Kildunne. That's how she plays.' Whenever I do feel a bit of pressure, it tends to bring out the best in me. And that's what happened against Bristol.

When I received the ball in my own half from a Bears clearance kick, I set off to run it back with my usual intent, before kicking ahead. Two Bristol defenders converged on the ball, and although I was in hot pursuit I didn't expect to reclaim possession. Fortunately, the ball bounced up perfectly for me to score.

If you watch a replay of that try, you can see the smile on my face when I realised what I'd done. I don't normally feel really happy for myself when I score a try. I'm more delighted that I've played a role in helping the team to try and win. But that Bristol score was different.

It was a try from more than 50 metres, yet also far more than that. It was my way of showing the trolls on social media exactly who I am.

15
New Opportunities

I spent Christmas 2025 at home in Yorkshire for some much-needed family time. The last two years had been so crazy, just non-stop. Being back in Riddlesden provided an invaluable reset and time to really process what I've achieved. Until that point, I simply hadn't had the chance. I spent New Year's Eve in Amsterdam with friends. I actually felt a bit emotional as the clock chimed midnight and I reflected on what had been the most incredible 12 months. Time is not something I'm blessed with much of these days. Opportunities I never thought would come my way have suddenly become a reality. Ever since our victory over Canada on 27 September 2025, life has been pretty much non-stop, with a string of different commercial offers. They have kept me very, very busy, alongside my No. 1 priority, which is training and playing.

In the eyes of many, I'm now seen as a poster girl for women's rugby. I'm still coming to terms with being recognised a lot more. That's been a big change. At the start of 2026, I went to the launderette to do some washing. If I'm out and about in public now and want to stay unrecognised, I'll often put a hood up. That's what I did that day. I had my hood up in

CHAPTER 15

the launderette and had started to sort out my clothes, when I realised this older gentleman was looking at me. 'Forgive me for staring at you, but you look really familiar,' he said. 'Do you get that a lot? You look very much like Ellie Kildunne.' I pulled my hood down and told the man it was me. He replied: 'Oh my God, I can't believe I've just met you in the launderette. Can I shake your hand please?'

It was a really lovely interaction, but it still blows my mind that people want to stop me and ask for a picture, a conversation or an autograph. Sometimes, though, I do find those encounters quite awkward. I'm very grateful to have the life I do now. There are so many positives to seeing your profile rise, but I'm still trying to navigate how to deal with it all. I think things really started to change for me in 2024, when I won World Rugby player of the year, and then accelerated going into the 2025 Six Nations. That was when cowboy hats and posters with my name on them became far more common. When we played Italy in York at the start of the Championship, I started on the bench and only got a few minutes at the end as a replacement. After the final whistle had gone, I was doing some extra running training with Flo Robinson and Jade Shekells, who had won their first caps, and May Campbell, who had won her second. I said to them: 'We'll do a lap after we've finished our running to meet the fans.' I wanted them to experience the incredible support we now get at Red Roses matches, before they went off to see their friends and families. As I went round the pitch with May, Flo and Jade, all the fans were shouting my name. I felt awkward because I wanted to share the moment with these teammates who were celebrating an incredibly special day in their careers. If I'm out with other players, and someone asks for a picture with only me in it, I still find it a little bit awkward. I've tried not to and I've got better at it, but I still do find those sorts of encounters a bit odd. I guess the bottom line is that, in my head, all the England players are equal. We all play in the same team and have shared in the same success.

I'm also aware that my friends value their privacy. I don't ever want what my life has become to be a problem of any kind for those closest to me. When I was in Amsterdam for New Year's Eve, I had a text from my agent Ben asking if I'd told anyone of my plans. He'd had an email from a journalist at a national newspaper asking if I was in the Dutch city. I had no idea what that could have been about, but the last thing I would have wanted was any intrusion on a trip I'd taken with friends.

I find this sort of stuff very tricky. During the World Cup, I read lots of articles speculating about my private life, mainly my relationship status. There was press coverage of me on holiday in Dubai after we'd won the tournament. I even read an article once that claimed my Harlequins and England teammate Lucy Packer is my girlfriend. Just for the record, I can confirm that's definitely not the case!

You're not prepared for any of this when you're making your way in professional sport, but I try to remind myself that while there are downsides to being in the public eye, they are outweighed by the positives. I'm determined to use it as a force for good. Women's rugby has exploded in popularity and I'm proud to have played my part in that.

CHAPTER 15

The way my life has changed can perhaps be best summed up by the fact that in 2021 I got the train into Twickenham on the same day as a men's England Six Nations game with Ireland. The train was full of England fans heading to the match, but I went unrecognised as I listened to my music while standing up in a packed carriage. Four years later, on the day of our World Cup final with Canada, there were street sellers on Whitton Road outside Allianz Stadium selling England scarves with my face and name on. That blew my mind when I found out.

Going into the World Cup, I was well aware that I'd put myself out there a bit more, and potentially increased the pressure on myself by widening my commercial work. After winning the final, I got more and more of those sorts of offers. I never would have thought I'd be made into a Barbie. But that is what has happened.

After the final, Ben messaged me telling me he had an update about a potential collaboration with the famous doll company. My first reaction was: 'I don't want a sponsorship deal with Barbie because, let's be honest, I'm more like Ken than Barbie! I didn't play with a Barbie growing up. I was too busy playing in the garden in Riddlesden.'

Ben told me that that wasn't the offer and that Barbie wanted to make a doll of little old me from West Yorkshire. It was a real pinch-me moment. Alongside USA star Ilona Maher, France's Nassira Konde and Portia Woodman-Wickliffe of New Zealand, I was one of four women's rugby players to have an imitation Barbie doll made of them.

In the end, the likeness of the doll to me was spot on. The hair on the first version they sent me wasn't quite right. But the second version, which incorporated my feedback, was brilliant. It even had my earrings, nose ring and physique. All the dolls reflected the different statures of the players.

It was another huge moment for women's rugby as a whole. I was honest with the people from the company about the fact that I didn't play with a Barbie as a child. But maybe part of the reason for that was because there wasn't a Barbie that looked like me when I was growing up. Now, hopefully, that's different. The dolls aren't on public sale. I believe there was only a single limited-edition doll made of each of us. And I'm not actually sure what happened to mine, but wherever it ends up in the future, I hope it stays with someone who is inspired by the story of England winning the World Cup.

One of the other more interesting offers I've had post-World Cup was to do a voiceover for Heathrow Airport. My voice was played over the Tannoy during the 2024 Christmas period, welcoming passengers to the airport and passing on festive wishes. It took a lot of planning and a whole day of recording, not to mention a big chunk of my time and energy. But it was completely different to rugby, and that's why I loved it doing it. This is the balance I'm trying to find now. I want to make the most of offers that come my way, but I also have to make sure it doesn't tire me out for training and matches.

The two separate parts of my life – rugby and non-rugby – are now heavily intertwined.

I've had to learn a lot very quickly about not putting too much pressure on myself. I'm really grateful to have an amazing support system around me.

CHAPTER 15

My weekly schedule still revolves around rugby. But my agent Ben helps me navigate everything else. I say to him before the start of a new week: 'What have I got on?' He tells me my movements and travel logistics. One of the things we always factor in is making sure I'm eating right. When I'm so busy, my ADHD means I focus heavily on whatever it is at the moment, and sometimes I can forget to eat as a result.

Since the World Cup, I've been to the *GQ* awards and been in the same room as people like the actors Cynthia Erivo and Pierce Brosnan. When we were there, my England teammate Sadia Kabeya turned to me and said: 'You have no idea the floor you're walking on.' That hit home. I feel hugely fortunate to be in the position I am. I was on the judging panel for the Pride of Britain awards. I also went to the event and handed out the awards on stage. Signing with Defender was pretty cool. I can't believe I'm driving around in a Defender now. It's certainly an upgrade from my first Volkswagen Polo! Defender let me customise my own car. I've gone for matte black on the outside and white on the inside.

One of the things I've enjoyed doing most was a talk at The Ned in London, which is a plush hotel. It was an event attended by 50 of the biggest insurance companies in the world. I was the lead speaker, which I didn't realise until I arrived. That brought some pressure with it, but the organisers told me they'd never sold as many tickets. I don't know anything about insurance. I'm not bothered about insurance. It doesn't interest me at all. But what does interest me is how can I use my knowledge and my experience to inspire people in their own worlds. I try to pass on what I've learned from rugby – whether that's leadership, teamwork, drive, sacrifice or anything else – to find common ground with others, who might not even know anything about the game I play. I loved doing the talk and got really good feedback, which has given me confidence to do more of them in the future. Life is all about gaining new experiences.

I've been close to burning out in the past six months, but the Christmas and New Year period gave me a priceless chance to reset. I was struggling to be consistent with my emotions, which was perhaps a telltale sign. I've really enjoyed being so busy and doing so many new things, but I'm also well aware that has only added pressure on me to perform. I know that if I'm doing all these different things away from rugby, I need to keep on playing well. If I don't, the inevitable criticism will start: 'Ellie is doing too much away from rugby and all the praise has gone to her head.' The more I do, the more eyes are going to be on me, and the more people will expect. I love that pressure. I need it because it gives me purpose.

Playing rugby and now winning the World Cup has totally changed my life in ways I still can't quite believe. But as much as many things have changed for me, I'd like to think I'm still very much the same person. I'm still just Ellie – a little weirdo from West Yorkshire. That's how I continue to feel, especially when I'm with the people that matter most to me. The last year has really opened my eyes to how important my family and close friends are, because no matter what happens in my life they will always be there.

CHAPTER 15

I've always tried to be different. I like to play and think differently to other players. And I like to look different. I'm not trying to be like anybody else and I never will. I'm loved most by those who understand fully who I am. I've never felt more loved and supported by those people. They're the ones who strip me back to Ellie from West Yorkshire. Not the Ellie who was second at Sports Personality of the Year and who has just been made an MBE. In many ways, everything I've achieved has come without me having much of a plan. I always knew I wanted to play rugby, but I'm winging it with everything else that has happened. In many areas of my life, I have absolutely no idea what I'm doing. I'm perfectly imperfect. But I wouldn't have it any other way.

16
The Future

When I first started playing for England in 2017, I never could have imagined I'd go on to achieve as much as I have so far. If I'm honest, at times I feel like I'm living someone else's life. The growth of the women's game as a whole has also been remarkable. When I made my Red Roses debut, there were no professional contracts for women's 15-a-side players and games were played in front of small crowds. I believed that we would get to where we are now at some point, but I didn't think we would reach this scale so quickly. Now, we've won a World Cup in front of a sold-out Allianz Stadium, and off the field things have also changed significantly, with greater commercial opportunities for female players.

In January 2026, the England squad got back together for the first time since the World Cup. The camp wasn't so much about training, it was more about reconnecting as a group and establishing what our next targets were. It was also a chance to welcome a number of new faces.

There were lots and lots of meetings, but also a final opportunity to mark winning the World Cup. On 14 January, the England team attended a Champions Ball at Grosvenor

CHAPTER 16

House in London, for a huge tournament celebration. It was an amazing evening, a fantastic celebration of all we'd achieved. The theme was gold – one which stressed a few of the girls out, including me as I prefer silver to gold.

After training, we all travelled into London in Hummers. It was a little bit of luxury, with the music blaring and a glass of champagne on the go. I know some people go to their school prom in a Hummer, but it was the first time I'd been in one of them. At Grosvenor House, we were all dressed to impress. There was a DJ and dancing. I had a couple of glasses of wine, but I was absolutely knackered by midnight.

There were three separate buses back to our team hotel in Surrey, slated for three different times – 10pm, midnight and 2am. I got on the middle bus and was very grateful to do so. I was so tired from talking all night. We all knew that the next day we had two very important appointments. We were marking our World Cup win with visits to Windsor Castle and No. 10 Downing Street.

There were a couple of sore heads knocking around that Thursday morning, but we had our hair and make-up done again and popped on the suits we'd worn at the World Cup. First, we went to Windsor Castle, where we met the Princess of Wales again. When we arrived, we found ourselves in one of the castle's main rooms. There was gold stuff everywhere! I hadn't really known what to expect, but I would just describe it as very royal. There was more champagne, fruit juices and a million and one different canapés on offer. Maddie Feaunati and I were stood next to each other and spent the time before the Princess arrived trying to imagine what it would be like if we lived in a castle.

Meeting the Princess once more was such a lovely moment. She's so genuine. One of the first things she said to us was: 'Have none of you brought your cowboy hats?' She remembered that from being in the changing room at Brighton after our World Cup win over Australia. I thought it was really nice that she added that personal touch.

The Princess told us her children have got into rugby. That was amazing to hear. I think it says everything about how good the values of rugby are that the royal family's next generation is playing the sport. How cool would it be if Kate's daughter Charlotte played for England one day?

After that, we got back on the bus and headed into London to visit Downing Street. No. 10 had laid on a celebration for us where we met Prime Minister Keir Starmer and Lisa Nandy, the Secretary of State for Culture, Media and Sport, who had been at the World Cup final. I'm not a very political person, but Lisa Nandy said she was very grateful for what we'd done, because one of her goals was to get rugby – and all sports – played more by people, especially girls. A lot of the girls were more focused on stroking Larry – the famous Downing Street cat. Most of them were saying, 'Oh, he's so cute.' Larry is a famous cat, but he's not a cute cat in my opinion. That's coming from a dog person, though.

Being at No. 10 was another surreal moment. My overriding thought was that it was smaller and cosier than I expected. I wasn't sure what to expect, but I remember thinking to myself: 'I could see myself living here!'

CHAPTER 16

In the midst of the drinks reception, we were allowed to look around. Ever the explorer, I was eager to make the most of what was likely a once-in-a-lifetime chance to take a snoop around what is probably the most famous address in England. As I took a walk, I saw a door and thought to myself: 'I wonder what's through there?' When I opened the door, there was another one immediately in front of it. The rest of the girls said: 'Surely you're not going to open that one too?' I said: 'I am!' It was at that point that someone came running over and I was told I couldn't enter. I guess I'll never know what room I was about to go into.

At the start of February 2026, a few weeks after visiting Windsor Castle and No. 10, I was invited to appear as a guest on *The Jonathan Ross Show* ahead of the men's Six Nations. I couldn't believe it when I was asked. The chance to do something like that came maybe once-in-lifetime, so I was keen to make the most of it to help grow the profile of the women's game. I was on the show alongside actor Hugh Bonneville, actor and rapper Riz Ahmed, stand-up comedian Harriet Kemsley and American singer Jason Derulo.

On the same night I recorded the show, I was also named *Sunday Times* Sportswoman of the Year for 2025 and the Red Roses were named Team of the Year. Speaking to guys like Bonneville and Derulo – who I would watch on TV – was just bizarre. I kept thinking to myself: 'As if this is happening! It's Jason Derulo!' I exchanged numbers with him after the show and I'm looking forward to staying in touch.

I don't exactly know what the future looks like for women's rugby. But I've got no doubt there is another level coming.

Whatever it is, I want it to exceed our wildest imaginations. I don't want to put a limit on how big the game could become.

For the England team, winning the 2025 World Cup on home soil was better than we all could ever have wished for. I can only hope for the same success at the next World Cup, which will be held in Australia in 2029. There are a few years to go until that tournament begins, and the visibility and accessibility that women's rugby now has is far, far higher than it was even three or four years ago. Of course, I want more girls to play rugby, for more people to come to England games and watch them on the television. I'd also like to see more financial investment into the female game. But, generally speaking, I just hope that it stays on this upwards trajectory.

For that to happen, the No. 1 thing the England team needs to do is to keep playing well. Yes, we've won a home World Cup, seven straight women's Six Nations and 33 matches in a row. But for the sport to carry on growing, we can't stop there. Everyone follows a success story and that's what we need to continue to be. I still have my World Cup medal on my bedside table. I keep it there because I lose things all the time. It's obviously very valuable to me, but I know that if I were to take it, or put it, somewhere else I'd probably forget it, or lose it. I've been asked why I don't wear it more often. You should feel how heavy it is! If I wore it more, I think I'd have to see the physio. Sometimes, when I'm getting ready to go out, I'll look for some jewellery by my bed and catch sight of the medal. But it's also a great reminder for me each day of what we achieved as an England team, and a source of motivation for the future too.

CHAPTER 16

Watching England win and entertain definitely keeps bringing people back to our matches. But a big thing for me is that rugby should be played in all schools and is available to all young boys and girls, not just those at private establishments who are able to invest money into it. I went to Woodhouse Grove School, which is renowned for rugby, but I was the first girl to play it there. I want the game to be normalised for girls. Also, we need to have a version of rugby that can be played in inner cities across the country, but also all around the world, even if access to equipment or coaches is limited. What that looks like, I'm not so sure – maybe a shorter version of the game like sevens or tag. Whatever it is, something needs to be done to increase participation.

I'm incredibly proud of where I'm from and I know people in Yorkshire are proud of me as well. I have a sign on the wall at home which reads 'Yorkshire born and bred'. But the reality was that for me to progress in rugby union, I had to move south to Hartpury, because there weren't the same opportunities in the north. I didn't have a team of the necessary standard to play for in my local area. I want to show young girls from across England, especially the north, that you can do great things. But I think that while there have undoubtedly been improvements, it's still the case that the chances to excel in women's rugby are far higher if you live in the south of England. Premiership Women's Rugby (PWR) is not only English rugby's top league for female players, but also the best in the world. But of the nine teams in the division, only one is from the north – Manchester club Sale Sharks. There are three sides from London alone, my team Harlequins, Saracens and Ealing. I've heard some people say Loughborough is in the north. As a Yorkshire girl, I can tell you for free that it definitely isn't!

To make rugby more accessible to girls in the north, I think we need to have more teams spread across the whole country. The key to this, I believe, is that we don't have to fall into sync with the men's teams. If you look at the PWR, there are sides like Ealing and Loughborough who aren't naturally associated with a men's PREM Rugby team. That's awesome. I think that's what could happen in the north, perhaps with an outfit created somewhere like Leeds or Doncaster. Just because the men's teams from Leeds and Doncaster aren't in the PREM doesn't mean that they can't develop a women's team, in my opinion.

It doesn't matter who you are or where you're from, the journey to where you want to be is never straightforward. That certainly applies to me. But I'd like to think I've shown young girls as well as boys that if you've got heart and desire and a passion to do something, you can find a way. That said, it's about maximising the drive you have by amplifying opportunities. If you're a girl and playing in a boys' team, it's about making sure you're not just stuck on the wing. That is what happened to me at times. If you're a good player and know the game, you should be put in a decision-making role, regardless of your gender. I think little things like that can help tackle the stigma that rugby is only for boys, and crush the stereotypes that cause girls to drop out when they're 12 or 13. This is a story I often hear, from both parents and kids. Clearly, the reasons for this can be complex, but I believe a major factor is that when girls go to secondary school they encounter new groups of friends who they want to fit in with. Puberty and body changes can also be a reason. I just think that if we normalise the fact that rugby's a sport that can be played whatever your gender, then that will go a long way. I'm a strong believer that you can achieve anything, as long as you've got the motivation to do so.

I've been with Harlequins since 2021 and, like every other PWR side, we're working hard to try and win the league title. To do that, we want to find consistency within the team and with our performances. We've probably been a little bit too inconsistent to compete with the best in the PWR in recent years. As competitive athletes, winning is everything. But as players in England, we also want to drive a league that's exciting and brings thousands of people to watch. We've played in front of huge crowds with the national side, the 81,885 who watched the 2025 World Cup final with Canada being the biggest. The PWR attendances aren't at that level yet, but they're definitely growing, and that's what we want to continue to see.

The PWR's quality and success is in large part down to significant investment from the RFU. You see that not only through the depth of English talent in the league, but also through the number of top foreign players who have come. USA superstar Ilona Maher and Ruahei Demant of New Zealand both playing for Bristol is a good example. Gloucester-Hartpury have been dominant for the past three seasons, but this year has been far more competitive. The standards are going to another level, both on and off the field. I think that's exciting. That's what people want.

THE FUTURE

At Harlequins, the culture is brilliant and the club has really helped develop different parts of my game. There was a time when I was actually thinking about leaving, but the reason I stayed was the girls and my connection with the coaches. I'm really glad that I did.

What drives me has changed over time. The past few years have all been about the World Cup. Now the World Cup is done, it can't be a driver for me any more. Fortunately, I've got so many other things to motivate me. I want to be the best player in the world again. Spending more time with my teammates – who I love so much – and making memories on and off the field is also a driver. Happiness is a big thing for me. You've got to enjoy what you do. When I was at Hartpury College, I ruined the last three months of my first year because I was so sad that my two friends Ella Wyrwas and Rosanna Moynihan in the year above were leaving. If I'd just stayed in the moment and found happiness in their company, I'd have enjoyed that time so much more. That's something I've learned with the benefit of experience.

New drivers come up out of nowhere for me all the time. Finishing second at Sports Personality of the Year has changed things again. It's reaffirmed to me I want other people to be inspired by the way I play rugby. That drive then switches from internal to external and that's okay. It doesn't mean I'm just being a people pleaser or that I'm playing for other people. It's just one part of my motivation recipe. I now know that new people are going to be watching me play rugby and I want to show them I'm worth the hype. I also want to show those people that the teams I play in are filled with many other inspirational role models.

CHAPTER 16

I haven't lacked motivation since the World Cup, but nailing down my new drivers has taken some time. The World Cup final was a bit like what I imagine your wedding day to be like. It was a big day we'd all set in our future, and we had a year or more to count down to it. Once it had gone, it took a bit of time to adjust. Coming back from the World Cup, I struggled a bit. I wanted Harlequins to do well and to use the momentum from the World Cup to keep the women's game growing. I wanted to continue to be the best player I could. In my brain, I've been arguing with myself about why I've not quite been right emotionally with my rugby. Why have I not been getting up for games as much? Why do I no longer feel the same joy when we win or sadness when we lose? But one thing that's really given me a new lease of life with Harlequins is joining the leadership group responsible for driving our attacking game.

I've got so many ideas and I want to keep on pushing people and improving. I am sure some of my teammates find me a nightmare because of that. I watch so much rugby. I know the game inside out, so joining the attack group was a natural step. That's something I've really enjoyed. Motivations change over time, but an overriding feeling I've always had is that I want to get to the end of my career and know I did everything I could have possibly done in the time I had.

As things stand, I'm currently very busy with my playing career and that has to be my full focus. I want to keep on pushing myself because I know that time in rugby can come and go very quickly. There's talk of all sorts of different things in the future, like the proposed breakaway league R360, which is now slated to begin in 2028. But all you can do as a player is focus on the here and now. The opportunities that have been put in front of the Red Roses players both before and after the 2025 World Cup have been amazing. When you become a sports star and your profile grows, other offers like *I'm a Celebrity... Get Me Out of Here!* and *Strictly Come Dancing* may well come along. I've got two left feet at the best of times, so I wouldn't say *Strictly* would be for me, although I do think it would make for good television. There'll be plenty of years after my career to get the dancing shoes on and give that a go. Right now, I'm fully focused on the progression of my game and the teams that I play for, so the talent shows I used to love watching as a child will have to wait for now.

Why would I ever want to stop playing rugby? It's so much fun. I want to keep going for as long as I possibly can. I love what I do. You can see the smile on my face when I play. I won't be able to do it for the rest of my life, so why not enjoy it while I've got the ball in my hand?

I've been very fortunate in my career so far to marry team success with personal accolades such as World Rugby player of the year in 2024, finishing second at BBC Sports Personality of the Year and being made an MBE. At the moment, I'm going wherever the wind takes me, all with the underlying belief that if I continue to try and make myself a better player, it'll take me further forward to more good things.

The first women's British & Irish Lions tour to New Zealand, in the summer of 2027, is going to be a milestone moment for the female game. Again, that's probably one of

CHAPTER 16

those things I didn't expect to happen. But then I have to catch myself and ask: 'Why not?' With the depth of women's rugby now, I think it's come at the right time. The Lions has existed for more than 100 years in the men's game. It's a team selected from players eligible for England, Ireland, Scotland and Wales, and every four years, they tour Australia, South Africa or New Zealand. If you're a player from the British Isles, selection for the Lions is widely seen as the pinnacle of your career.

To be a part of the first women's Lions would be amazing, but it's not my main focus right now because it's still a year or more away. If I focus solely on something that's going to take place in 2027, I risk watching a year or more of my career slip past. If I don't stay in the moment, I won't even be in the place to be selected, because I won't be good enough. The same applies to the prospect of playing sevens again at the 2028 Olympics. It's something I would love to do, but I can't afford to get distracted by long-term goals.

On a personal level, I think I can still improve my individual game. I want to be faster. I want to be stronger. I want to be more confident in my tackles. I want to be a better kicker. I want to be more tactical. There is still so much more to come from me. I don't think I even played my best game at the 2025 World Cup. There were plenty of good moments, like the two tries in the semi-final against France and the score in the final against Canada. But how exciting is it that we won the tournament and there is still so much more to come? There was one moment in the final with Canada where I chipped the ball on the right side of one of their players, but I should have done it on the left because that's where there was more space. The fact I didn't do that correctly still keeps me up at night. Until I'm in another World Cup final, or in the same position again, I will carry on thinking about it.

I'm driven to keep my personal game and women's rugby overall progressing. You've got to have that self-motivation and find little wins to keep you going. It can be hard at times when you're not chasing something like a World Cup or a Lions tour. But those big tournaments aren't what gets me out of bed in the morning. What gets me out of bed is my love for the game, which continues to grow day by day. I didn't realise until recently that interacting with fans while I'm playing makes me love it. The way that I can turn around after scoring a try and be embraced by my teammates is why I love it. The fact I can see cowboy hats in the crowds is why I love it. So, I've got to keep on doing the fitness, the skills and the gym work, so that I can score tries and turn around, see the girls running at me and see the happiness that it brings them.

One of the things I'm very aware of as an England women's player today is that the opportunities available to me both in rugby and off the field are very, very different to those available to the generations that came before. As Red Roses, we say we play not only for those who will follow in our footsteps, but also for those who wore our shirts previously. It's great to see what's happening now and I'm hoping I've got another 10 years or more before I even have to think about retiring.

In the past, England's women's rugby players – as well as those from other sports – have at times been forced to choose

CHAPTER 16

between their careers and the prospect of motherhood. But the advances in the women's game now mean that as an England player I am entitled to 26 weeks of fully paid maternity leave, as well as funds for children to travel to games. The RFU's 2023 update to their maternity policy needed to happen and, in truth, was probably overdue. I'm not ready for children right now. No. 1, you need a partner to have a child and I'm not in that position at the moment. But I'd love to have them one day, whether that's during my playing career or not. I guess once you get to the point where you know it's the right time, you just go with it. It's been inspirational to me to see my teammates Abbie Ward and Marlie Packer have their children Hallie and Oliver, and continue to be international rugby players. Another of my England teammates, Lark Atkin-Davies, is also expecting a baby this year. They are showing there is a pathway to be both a mother and a player, and breaking new boundaries in doing so.

I've read a lot of commentary in rugby about the need for the game to grow the profile of its leading players, both men's and women's. I think that's hugely important because for the sport to grow, it needs individuals to stand out from the crowd. It's a really exciting time because, as players, we can now show our personalities; we're no longer just the numbers on the backs of our shirts.

Growing up, I was very much a people pleaser. I was constantly trying to mould myself around others. In the past few years, my game and my personality have developed because I'm authentically myself. There are going to be people who don't like you but then there are going to be so many people who do, and they're your people. You don't need to seek approval by meeting the expectations of others, because you'll get found out at some point. I wish I'd learned that earlier, because the friendships I've got now are so beautiful. I'm loved for who I truly am, not a façade.

At the end of 2025, I did a commercial appearance for England sponsor O2 with Henry Pollock, who has quickly become a star in the men's game. I think Pollock is very misunderstood. Some people have criticised him for perhaps being cocky or arrogant. They think he might be a bit of a showboat. But he's a really nice guy and gives off a younger brother vibe. I got on with him when we talked, and I came away from our conversation thinking that people have misconceptions about him. I think the persona he shows to the public is exactly what he's like in private. He's not faking anything and it really reminded me of what we stand for in the Red Roses – the ability and the freedom to express yourself authentically.

With England, we want to continue to be successful. We'll have to do it without my now former back-three partner Abby Dow. Abby retired at the end of last year to pursue a career in engineering – a subject which she is hugely passionate about. Abby, Jess Breach and I have played so much of our rugby together and scored so many tries that we became well-versed in combining together on the field. We will miss Abby, but time waits for no one and professional rugby is always changing. All teams are constantly evolving, and this England side is no different.

I started 2026 having been very, very lucky to have won all but two of my 57 games for my country. My only losses have

CHAPTER 16

been the 2022 World Cup final to New Zealand and a 2018 Six Nations defeat by France. In those 57 caps, I've scored 45 tries, but I wouldn't be able to record such statistics without the help of my teammates. And, again, scoring tries is only a by-product of delivering my best on the field, and that's something I'll never stop trying to do.

As women's rugby has grown, its visibility and accessibility has definitely progressed to heights that we players can barely believe. I'm determined to ride the wave and enjoy every minute. But I don't want to ever feel like I've achieved it all. If I get to that position, I think I'll feel bored. I've won Six Nations titles and Grand Slams, a World Cup, been named World Rugby player of the year, finished second in the BBC Sports Personality of the Year and been awarded an MBE. I'm a lass from Yorkshire who has achieved more than she ever thought possible. But at the same time, there is far more to come from me in the years to follow.

Watch this space. Buckle up, cowboys. I'm only just getting started.

Acknowledgements

Writing this book has been just like how I imagine therapy to be. Reliving my journey from Keighley Albion to England, and all the ups and downs I've experienced along the way, has been a surprisingly cathartic process. When I set out to chart my career so far, I wanted to produce a book that appealed not only to rugby fans but to those who have never watched a minute of the sport. The reason for that was because I want my story to inspire everyone, not just those who love the sport I play. I also think that by being honest about the experiences I've had, I can help anyone, in any walk of life. I really hope that proves to be the case.

There is still so much more to come from me in the years ahead. But me getting to this point wouldn't have been possible without the help of so many people. My biggest thank you goes to my family. My mum Alison, dad Nigel and brother Sam – also known as 'my Sweens' – have always been and continue to be the ones who believe in me the most. When I first started playing rugby as the only girl in boys' teams in West Yorkshire, my parents and Sam were at every match – giving up hours and hours of their time to take me to and from matches and training. Their commitment to my rugby career remains absolute, and to this day, they still come to all of my England games.

ACKNOWLEDGEMENTS

I owe everything to them for what they've done for me. What's been brilliant for us as a family is that both Sam and I have gone on to play rugby at the highest level. Sam is currently with Ampthill in the RFU Championship and has also played sevens for Great Britain. As siblings, we each know what the other is going through and are able to provide the right sort of support when it's needed. One of the proudest moments we've had as a family was when Sam and I both played sevens for Great Britain at the same tournament in Germany.

I have to thank so many people who have played integral parts in how my rugby has progressed. From my first coaches John Normington, Dean Brookes and Craig Livock at Keighley Albion, through to Simon Middleton and then John Mitchell, who have coached me with England, and everyone in-between, I am hugely grateful for their help, guidance and expertise.

Rugby is a team game. Without my teammates, I would not have been able to have achieved any of the things I have. My thanks go to everyone I have played alongside at Gloucester-Hartpury, Wasps, Harlequins and England in 15-a-side rugby – for the bonds and friendships I've made. The same applies to the girls who were my sevens colleagues, both with England and Great Britain.

To my friends and loved ones, thank you for listening to my crazy ideas, putting up with the chaos, and even cleaning my boots. You know who you are.

Ben Lewitt is my agent in name only. In the last year or more, as my life has changed and become incredibly hectic, he

ACKNOWLEDGEMENTS

has also acted as a friend and confidant; and at times as my personal assistant. His advice and support have been invaluable. Thank you, Ben.

To Jacqui Sommerville, thank you for always reminding me to live life to the fullest and to love and spread happiness in every room I walk into.

I am very grateful to everyone at Ebury Publishing for their help in producing this book. Thanks to Lorna Russell, Jasmin Kaur, Lucy Brown and Ellenor Jermyn for your expertise. A big thank you to my ghostwriter Alex Bywater. Being so honest about some areas of my life was tough, but Alex has seen large parts of my career in person, which meant I felt comfortable talking to him. I really enjoyed the process.

Lastly, but most importantly, thank you to you – the readers and fans of women's rugby. Without you, I wouldn't be where I am today. The same applies to the female game as a whole. Please keep supporting and coming to matches. Women's rugby has exploded in popularity. Together, we've smashed through the barriers the doubters thought we'd never reach, let alone break. Let's continue to do that and look forward to an even brighter future.

Image Credits

Image Section Two

Francesco Scaccianoce – World Rugby / Contributor / Getty Images

(Image 10)

Molly Darlington – World Rugby / Contributor / Getty Images

(Image 16)

Bob Bradford – CameraSport / Contributor / Getty Images

(Image 17)

WPA Pool / Pool / Getty Images

(Image 21)